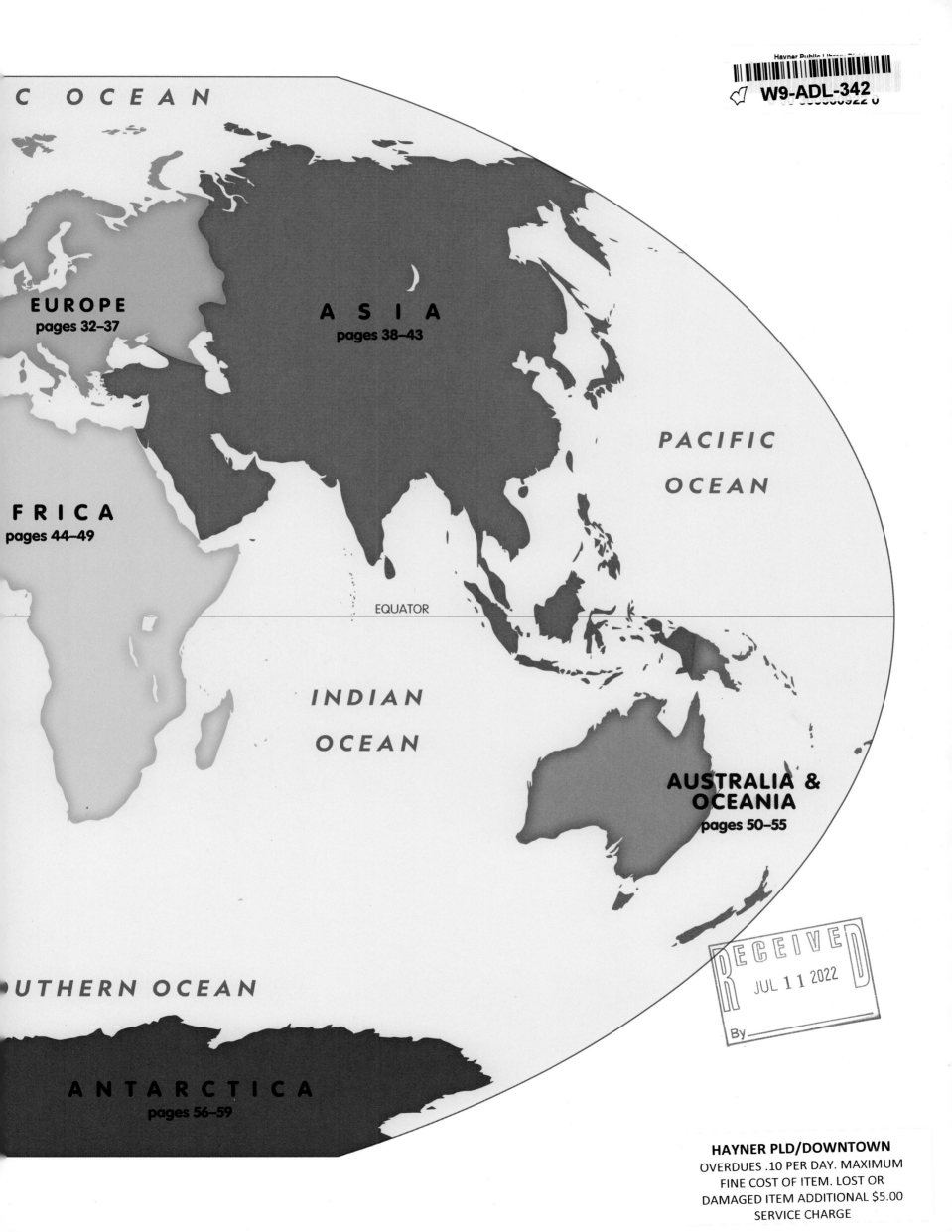

C OCEAN

EUROPE
pages 32–37

ASIA
pages 38–43

FRICA
pages 44–49

PACIFIC

OCEAN

EQUATOR

INDIAN

OCEAN

AUSTRALIA &
OCEANIA
pages 50–55

UTHERN OCEAN

ANTARCTICA
pages 56–59

NATIONAL GEOGRAPHIC KiDS

BEGINNER'S WORLD ATLAS

NATIONAL GEOGRAPHIC
WASHINGTON, D.C.

Contents

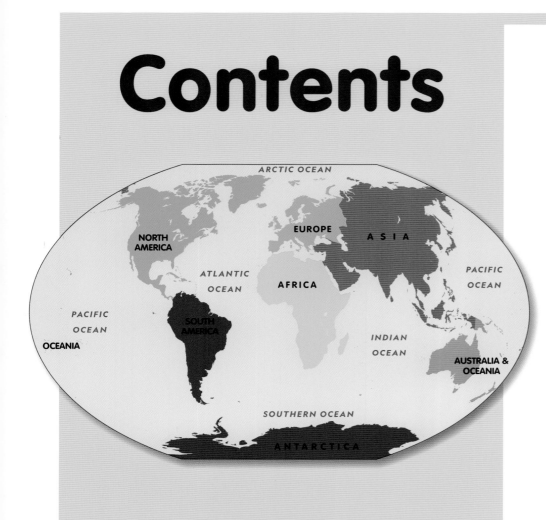

Understanding Your World

This atlas uses maps and photographs to reveal the wonderful diversity of people, cultures, and the natural world that makes each place on Earth unique. Look for examples of diversity in the land and the people, ranging from traditional to modern lifestyles and from animals in the wild to bustling cities.

Making the Round Earth Flat

From your front door Earth probably looks flat. If you could travel into space like an astronaut, you would see that Earth is a giant ball with blue oceans, greenish brown land, and white clouds. Even in space you can see only the part of Earth facing you. To see the whole planet at one time, you need a map. Maps take the round Earth and make it flat, so you can see all of it at once.

Earth in Space
From space you can see that Earth is round, with oceans, land, and clouds. But you can see only half of Earth at one time.

Earth as a Globe

A globe is a tiny model of Earth that you can put on a stand or hold in your hand. You still can't see all of Earth at one time. You have to turn the globe to see the other side.

Earth on Paper

If you could peel a globe like an orange, you could make Earth flat, but there would be spaces between the pieces. Mapmakers stretch the land and the water at the top and bottom to fill in the spaces. This is how a map lets you see the whole world all at once.

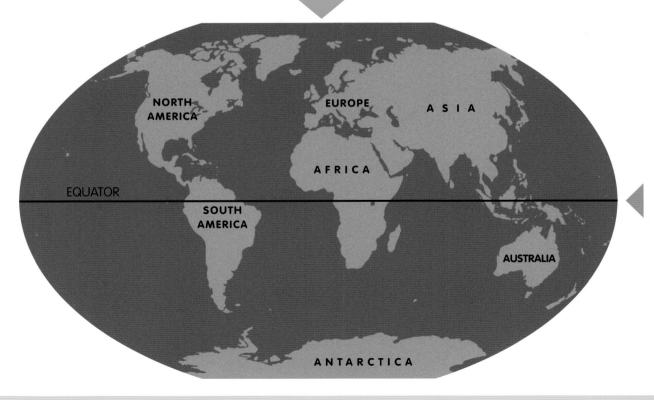

NORTH AMERICA

EUROPE

ASIA

AFRICA

EQUATOR

SOUTH AMERICA

AUSTRALIA

ANTARCTICA

The Equator

The Equator is an imaginary line around Earth's middle. It divides the world into two halves—the Northern Hemisphere and the Southern Hemisphere.

What Is a Map?

A map is a drawing of a place as it looks from above. It is flat, and it is smaller than the place it shows. A map can help you find where you are and where you want to go.

Mapping your backyard ...

... from the ground

From your backyard you see everything in front of you straight on. You have to look up to see your roof and the tops of trees. You can't see what's in front of your house.

... from higher up

From higher up you look down on things. You can see the tops of trees and things in your yard and the yards of other houses in your neighborhood.

Finding Places on the Map

A map can help you get where you want to go. You can read a map by looking at the compass rose, a scale, and a key.

A compass rose helps you travel in the right direction. It tells you where north (N), south (S), east (E), and west (W) are on your map.

Some maps have only a north arrow.

0	300	600 miles
0	450	900 kilometers

In the scale above, the upper bar represents distance in miles. The lower bar represents distance in kilometers. You can use a scale to figure out the actual distance between two places on Earth.

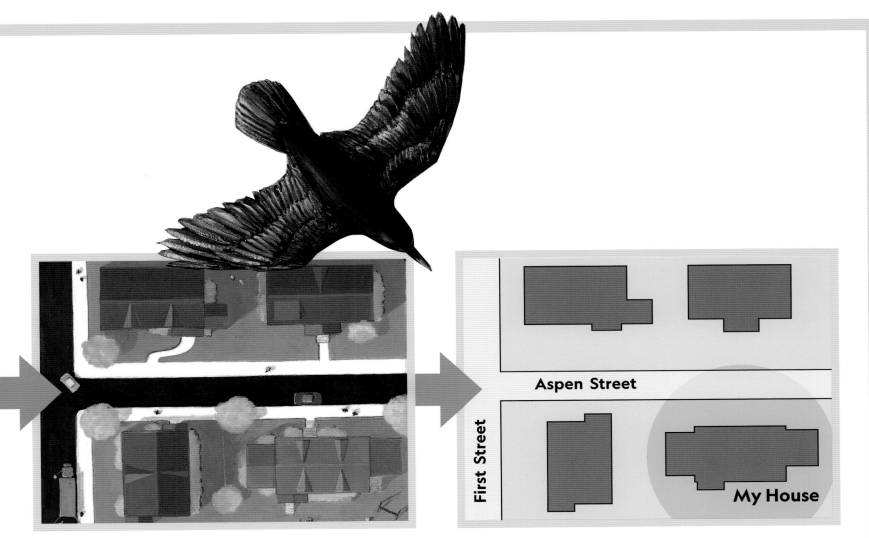

... from a bird's-eye view

If you were a bird flying directly overhead, you would see only the tops of things. You wouldn't see walls, tree trunks, tires, or feet.

... on a map

A map looks at places from a bird's-eye view. But it uses drawings called symbols to show things that don't move, such as these houses.

A map key helps you understand symbols and colors used on the map. The symbols and colors can show things like mountains, deserts, grasslands, or boundaries.

Map Key
- Mountain
- Desert
- Coniferous forest
- Deciduous forest
- Rainforest
- Grassland
- Wetland
- Tundra
- Volcano
- Dry salt lake
- — Europe-Asia boundary

What This Atlas Will Teach You

You hold the world in your hands as you turn the pages of this atlas. Physical maps will show you natural features, and political maps will show you countries and other places created by people.

Desert, North America

Coral reef, Pacific Ocean

ARCTIC OCEAN

NORTH AMERICA

EUROPE

ASIA

ATLANTIC OCEAN

PACIFIC OCEAN

AFRICA

PACIFIC OCEAN

EQUATOR

SOUTH AMERICA

INDIAN OCEAN

AUSTRALIA

SOUTHERN OCEAN

ANTARCTICA

THE PHYSICAL WORLD

 Land regions You will find out what kinds of land cover a continent. Does it have mountains and deserts? If so, where are they?

 Water You will learn about a continent's major lakes, rivers, and waterfalls. You'll see that some continents have more water than others.

Climate Climate is the weather of a place over many years. Some continents are colder and wetter or hotter and drier than others.

 Plants You'll discover what kinds of plants grow on a particular continent.

 Animals Continents each have certain kinds of animals that are adapted to survive in that location. Did you know that Asia is the only place on Earth where tigers live in the wild?

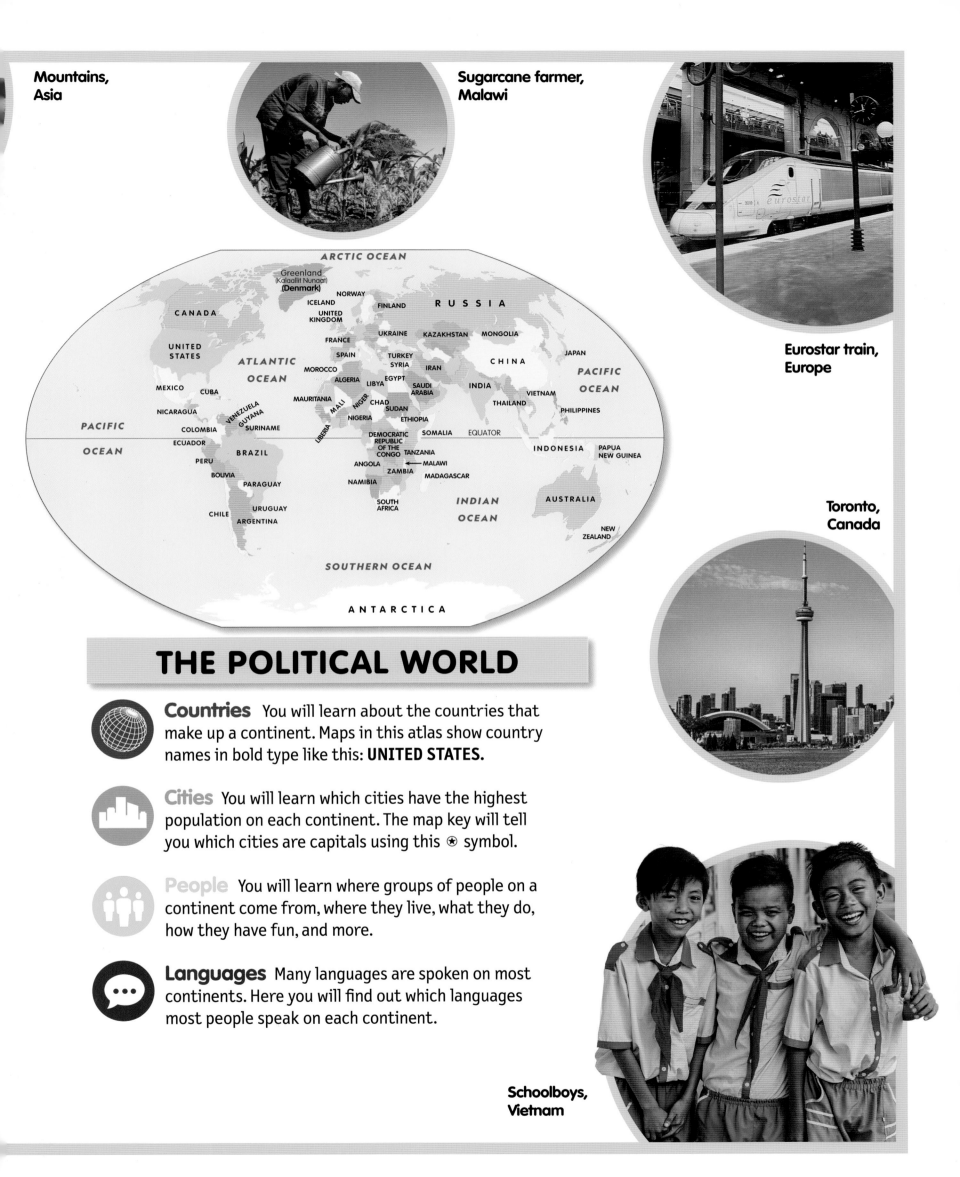

Mountains, Asia

Sugarcane farmer, Malawi

Eurostar train, Europe

Toronto, Canada

ARCTIC OCEAN

Greenland
(Kalaallit Nunaat)
(Denmark)

NORWAY

ICELAND
UNITED
KINGDOM

FINLAND

RUSSIA

CANADA

UKRAINE   KAZAKHSTAN   MONGOLIA

FRANCE
UNITED
STATES

SPAIN   TURKEY
             SYRIA   IRAN

CHINA

JAPAN

ATLANTIC
OCEAN

MOROCCO
ALGERIA   LIBYA   EGYPT

PACIFIC
OCEAN

MEXICO   CUBA

SAUDI
ARABIA

INDIA

VIETNAM

MAURITANIA   MALI   NIGER   CHAD   SUDAN

THAILAND

PHILIPPINES

NICARAGUA

VENEZUELA
GUYANA
SURINAME

NIGERIA

ETHIOPIA

PACIFIC

COLOMBIA
ECUADOR

LIBERIA

DEMOCRATIC
REPUBLIC
OF THE
CONGO

SOMALIA   EQUATOR

OCEAN

PERU

BRAZIL

TANZANIA

INDONESIA   PAPUA
             NEW GUINEA

ANGOLA   ← MALAWI

BOLIVIA

ZAMBIA   MADAGASCAR

PARAGUAY

NAMIBIA

CHILE   URUGUAY
ARGENTINA

SOUTH
AFRICA

INDIAN

OCEAN

AUSTRALIA

NEW
ZEALAND

SOUTHERN OCEAN

ANTARCTICA

THE POLITICAL WORLD

Countries You will learn about the countries that make up a continent. Maps in this atlas show country names in bold type like this: **UNITED STATES.**

Cities You will learn which cities have the highest population on each continent. The map key will tell you which cities are capitals using this ✹ symbol.

People You will learn where groups of people on a continent come from, where they live, what they do, how they have fun, and more.

Languages Many languages are spoken on most continents. Here you will find out which languages most people speak on each continent.

Schoolboys, Vietnam

The Physical World

A physical map uses symbols and colors to show where mountains, deserts, forests, and other natural features of the land are.

The map key tells the meaning of the colors and symbols used on the map.

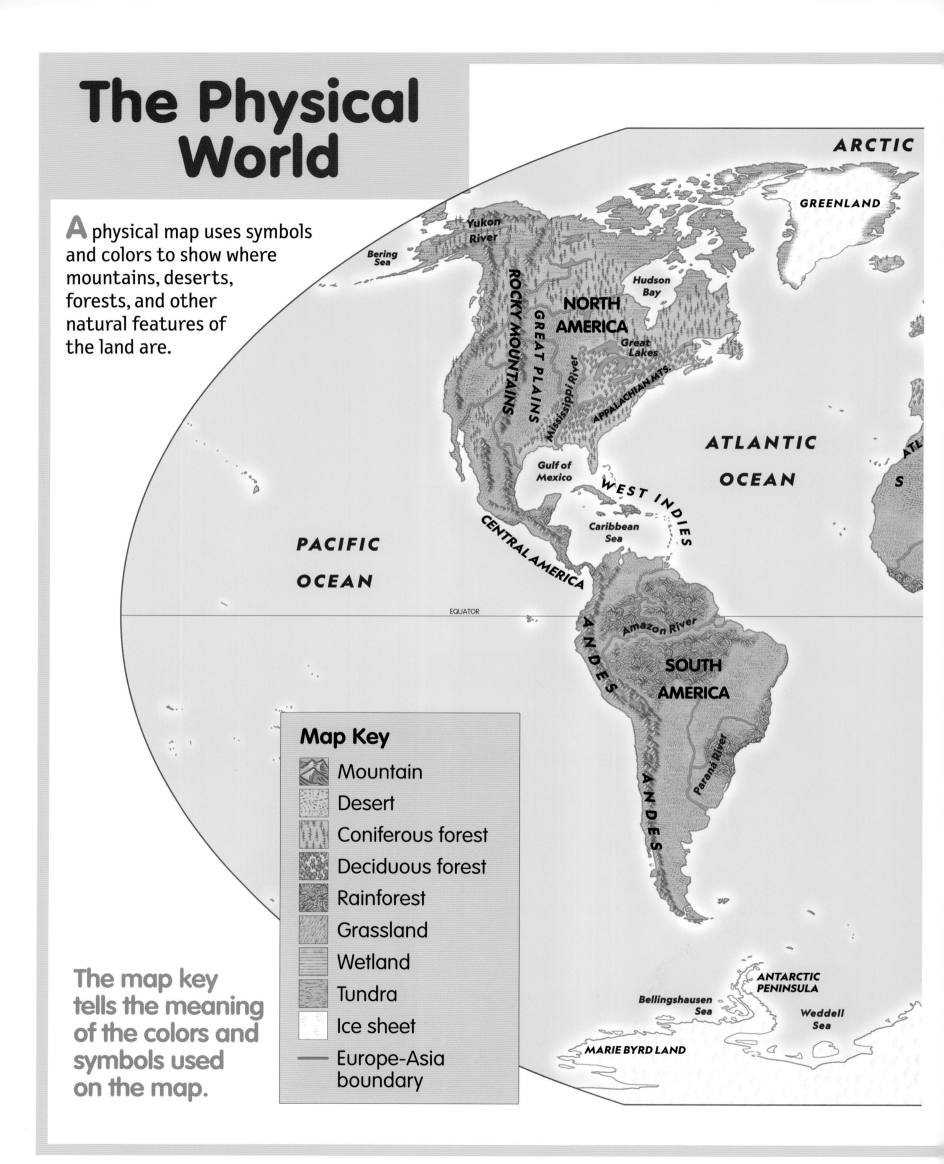

Map Key

- Mountain
- Desert
- Coniferous forest
- Deciduous forest
- Rainforest
- Grassland
- Wetland
- Tundra
- Ice sheet
- — Europe-Asia boundary

ARCTIC

GREENLAND

Bering Sea

Yukon River

NORTH AMERICA

ROCKY MOUNTAINS

GREAT PLAINS

Mississippi River

Hudson Bay

Great Lakes

APPALACHIAN MTS.

Gulf of Mexico

WEST INDIES

Caribbean Sea

ATLANTIC OCEAN

ATL

S

CENTRAL AMERICA

PACIFIC OCEAN

EQUATOR

ANDES

Amazon River

SOUTH AMERICA

Paraná River

ANTARCTIC PENINSULA

Bellingshausen Sea

Weddell Sea

MARIE BYRD LAND

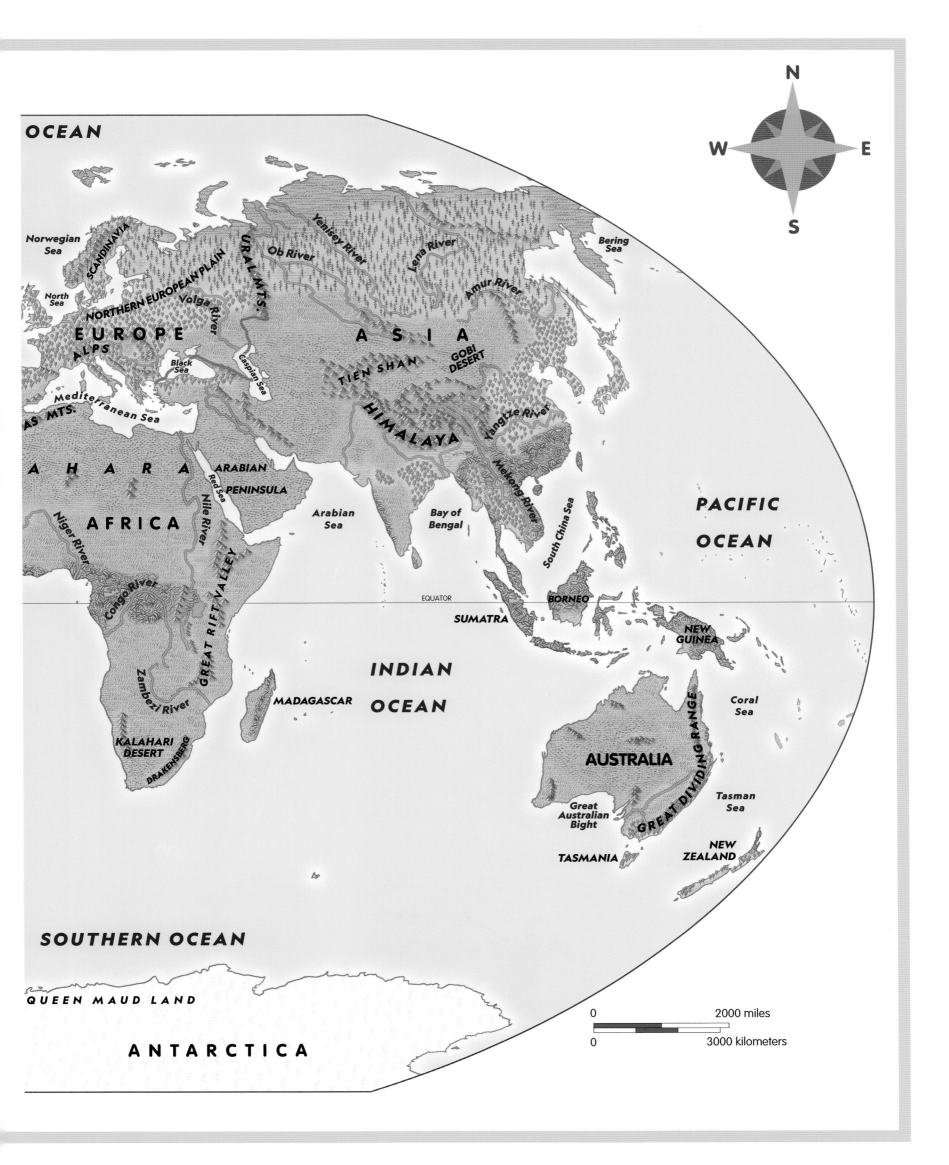

OCEAN

N
W E
S

Norwegian
Sea

North
Sea

SCANDINAVIA

NORTHERN EUROPEAN PLAIN

Volga River

URAL MTS.

Ob River

Yenisey River

Lena River

Amur River

Bering
Sea

EUROPE

ALPS

Black
Sea

Caspian Sea

ASIA

TIEN SHAN

GOBI
DESERT

HIMALAYA

Yangtze River

AS MTS.

Mediterranean Sea

SAHARA

ARABIAN
PENINSULA

Red Sea

Nile River

Arabian
Sea

Bay of
Bengal

Mekong River

South China Sea

PACIFIC

OCEAN

AFRICA

Niger River

Congo River

GREAT RIFT VALLEY

EQUATOR

SUMATRA

BORNEO

NEW
GUINEA

INDIAN

OCEAN

MADAGASCAR

Coral
Sea

Zambezi River

KALAHARI
DESERT

DRAKENSBERG

AUSTRALIA

GREAT DIVIDING RANGE

Tasman
Sea

Great
Australian
Bight

NEW
ZEALAND

TASMANIA

SOUTHERN OCEAN

QUEEN MAUD LAND

ANTARCTICA

0   2000 miles

0   3000 kilometers

The Physical World Close Up

Earth's surface is made up of land and water. The biggest landmasses are called continents. All seven continents are named on this map. Islands are smaller pieces of land that are completely surrounded by water. Greenland is the largest island. A peninsula is land that is almost entirely surrounded by water. Europe has lots of peninsulas.

Oceans are the largest bodies of water on Earth. Can you find all five oceans? Lakes are bodies of water surrounded by land, like the Great Lakes, in North America. A river is a large stream that flows into a lake or an ocean. The Nile, in Africa, is the longest river.

These are Earth's main physical features. But continents also have mountains, deserts, forests, and many other physical features. The map symbols on these pages show some of the features that will appear on the physical maps in this atlas. Each symbol is followed by a brief description that explains its meaning. There is also a photograph so you can see what each feature looks like in the real world.

ARCTIC

GREENLAND

NORTH AMERICA

ROCKY MOUNTAINS

Mississippi River

Great Lakes

APPALACHIAN MTS.

Gulf of Mexico

Caribbean Sea

ATLANTIC OCEAN

ATLAS

S A

PACIFIC OCEAN

EQUATOR

ANDES

Amazon River

SOUTH AMERICA

ANDES

ANDES

Mountain
Land rising at least 1,000 feet (305 m) above Earth's surface

Desert
Very dry land that can be hot or cold and sandy or rocky

Coniferous forest
Forest with trees that have seed cones and often needlelike leaves

OCEAN
EUROPE
ALPS
Volga River
URAL MTS.
EUROPE-ASIA BOUNDARY
ASIA
Gobi Desert
HIMALAYA
Yangtze River
Mediterranean Sea
MTS.
HARA
AFRICA
Nile River
PACIFIC OCEAN
EQUATOR
INDIAN OCEAN
AUSTRALIA
GREAT DIVIDING RANGE
SOUTHERN OCEAN
ANTARCTICA
0 2000 miles
0 3000 kilometers

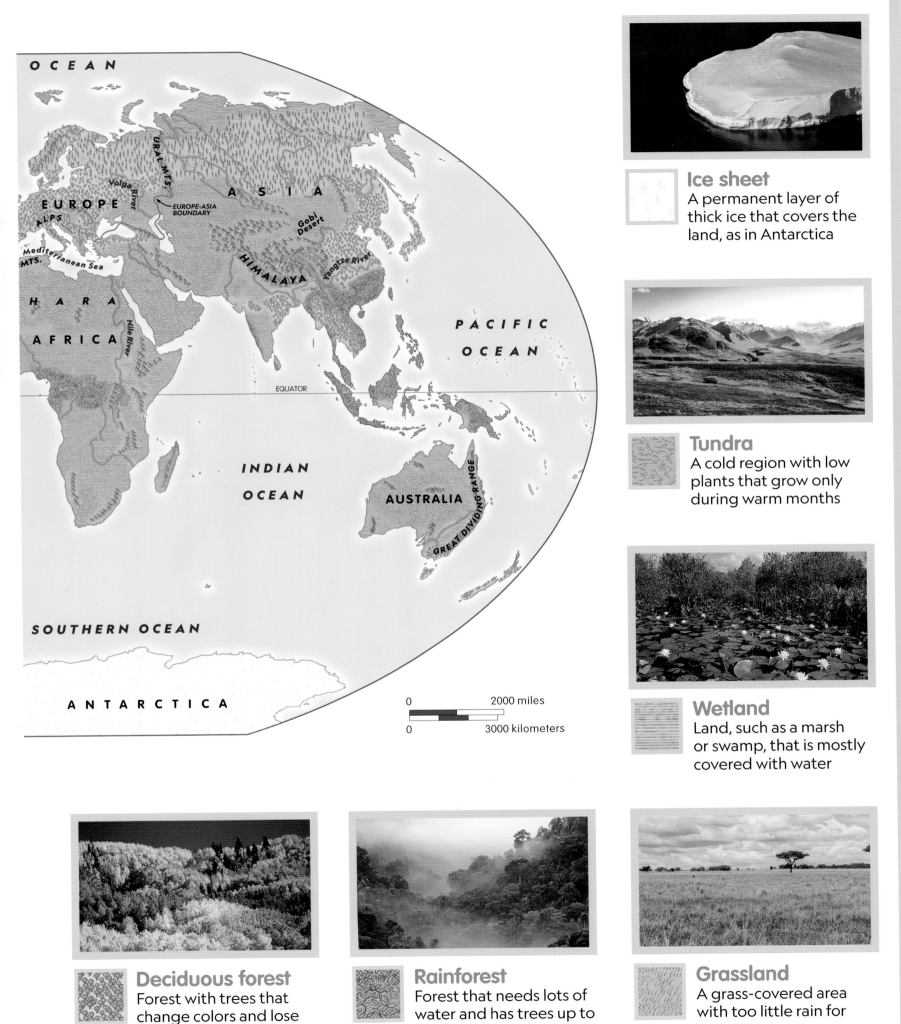

Ice sheet
A permanent layer of thick ice that covers the land, as in Antarctica

Tundra
A cold region with low plants that grow only during warm months

Wetland
Land, such as a marsh or swamp, that is mostly covered with water

Deciduous forest
Forest with trees that change colors and lose leaves in the fall

Rainforest
Forest that needs lots of water and has trees up to 200 feet (61 m) tall

Grassland
A grass-covered area with too little rain for many trees to grow

The Political World

Political maps show boundaries, places where people live, and other human features. This map names countries and territories of the world.

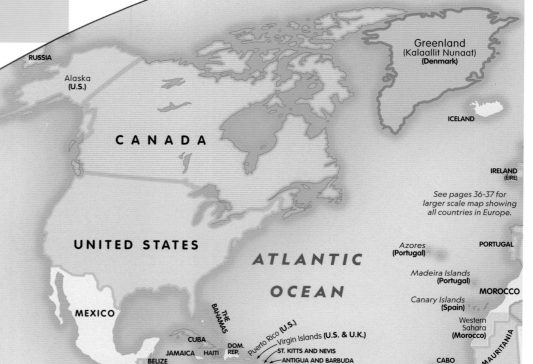

A R C

Greenland
(Kalaallit Nunaat)
(Denmark)

ICELAND

IRELAND
(ÉIRE)

See pages 36-37 for larger scale map showing all countries in Europe.

CANADA

UNITED STATES

ATLANTIC

OCEAN

RUSSIA

Alaska
(U.S.)

Azores
(Portugal)

PORTUGAL

Madeira Islands
(Portugal)

MOROCCO

Canary Islands
(Spain)

Western
Sahara
(Morocco)

MAURITANIA

MEXICO

THE BAHAMAS

CUBA

Puerto Rico (U.S.)

Virgin Islands (U.S. & U.K.)

ST. KITTS AND NEVIS

ANTIGUA AND BARBUDA

JAMAICA HAITI DOM. REP.

BELIZE

HONDURAS

DOMINICA

CABO VERDE

GUATEMALA

ST. LUCIA

SENEGAL

EL SALVADOR

NICARAGUA

GRENADA

BARBADOS

THE GAMBIA

ST. VINCENT AND THE GRENADINES

GUINEA-BISSAU

GUINEA

COSTA RICA

TRINIDAD AND TOBAGO

SIERRA LEONE

LIBERIA

PANAMA

VENEZUELA

GUYANA

SURINAME

CÔTE D'IVOIRE
(IVORY COAST)

Hawaii
(U.S.)

COLOMBIA

French Guiana
(France)

Kiritimati
(Kiribati)

PACIFIC

EQUATOR

Galápagos Islands
(Ecuador)

ECUADOR

OCEAN

Marquesas Islands
(France)

PERU

BRAZIL

ATLANTIC

SAMOA

American Samoa
(U.S.)

French Polynesia
(France)

BOLIVIA

OCEAN

TONGA

PARAGUAY

ABBREVIATIONS

Arm.	Armenia
Azer.	Azerbaijan
Belg.	Belgium
Bos. & Her.	Bosnia and Herzegovina
Dom. Rep.	Dominican Republic
Est.	Estonia
Latv.	Latvia
Lith.	Lithuania
Lux.	Luxembourg
Neth.	Netherlands
N. Mac.	North Macedonia
N.Z.	New Zealand
Slovn.	Slovenia
Switz.	Switzerland
U.A.E.	United Arab Emirates
U.K.	United Kingdom
U.S.	United States

CHILE

URUGUAY

ARGENTINA

Chatham Islands
(N.Z.)

Falkland Islands
(Islas Malvinas)
(U.K.)

South Georgia
(U.K.)

Colors make it easy to see the size and shape of each country.

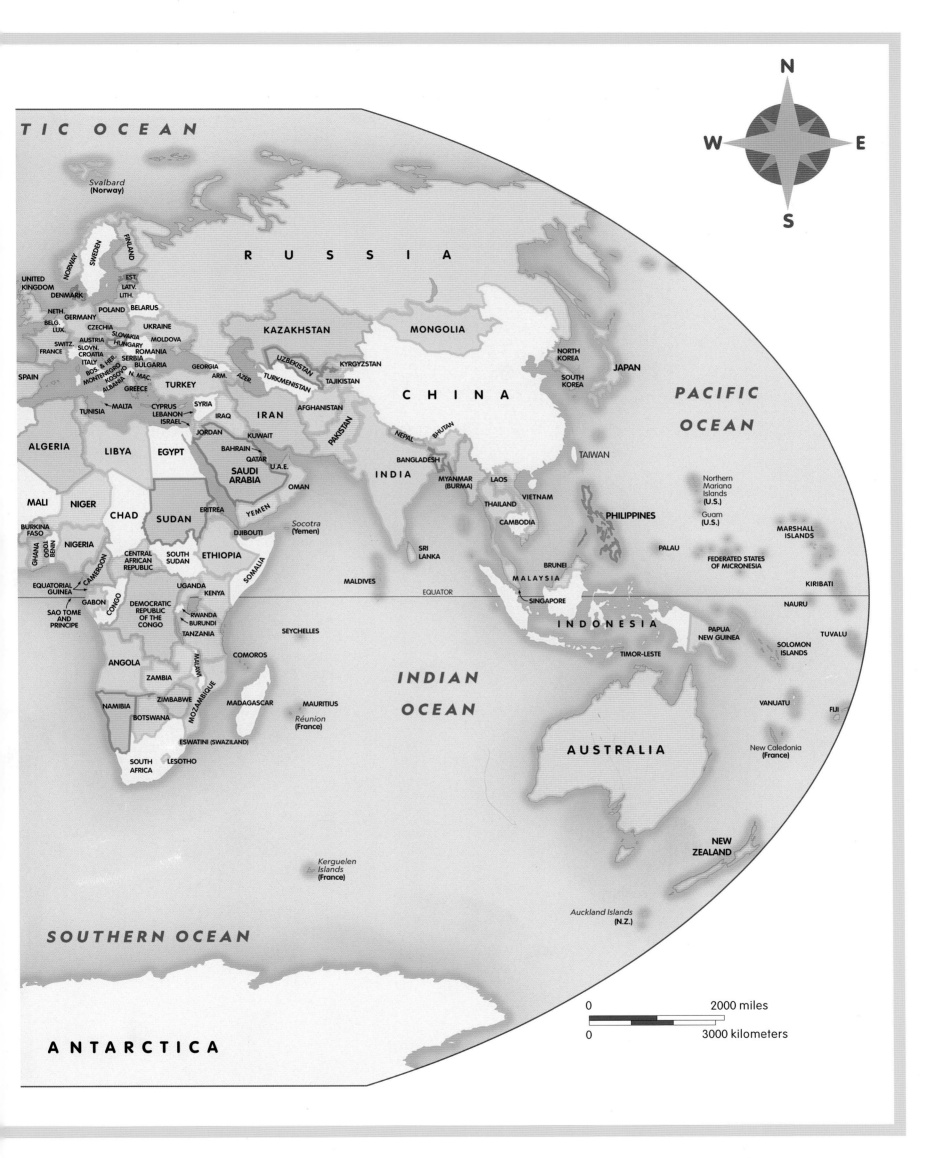

TIC OCEAN

Svalbard
(Norway)

NORWAY
SWEDEN
FINLAND

UNITED
KINGDOM
DENMARK
EST.
LATV.
LITH.

NETH.
BELG.
LUX.
GERMANY
POLAND
BELARUS

CZECHIA
SWITZ.
FRANCE
AUSTRIA
SLOVN.
ITALY
SLOVAKIA
HUNGARY
UKRAINE
MOLDOVA
ROMANIA

SPAIN
BOS. & HER.
MONTENEGRO
KOSOVO
ALBANIA
SERBIA
BULGARIA
N. MAC.
GREECE
GEORGIA
ARM.
AZER.

TUNISIA
MALTA
CYPRUS
LEBANON
ISRAEL
SYRIA
IRAQ
JORDAN
TURKEY

ALGERIA
LIBYA
EGYPT

MALI
NIGER
CHAD
SUDAN

BURKINA
FASO
NIGERIA

GHANA
TOGO
BENIN

EQUATORIAL
GUINEA
CAMEROON
CENTRAL
AFRICAN
REPUBLIC
SOUTH
SUDAN
ETHIOPIA

GABON
CONGO
DEMOCRATIC
REPUBLIC
OF THE
CONGO
UGANDA
KENYA
SOMALIA

SAO TOME
AND
PRINCIPE
RWANDA
BURUNDI
TANZANIA

ANGOLA
MALAWI
ZAMBIA

NAMIBIA
ZIMBABWE
MOZAMBIQUE

BOTSWANA

SOUTH
AFRICA
LESOTHO
ESWATINI (SWAZILAND)

COMOROS
MADAGASCAR
SEYCHELLES

MAURITIUS
Réunion
(France)

RUSSIA

KAZAKHSTAN
MONGOLIA

UZBEKISTAN
KYRGYZSTAN

TURKMENISTAN
TAJIKISTAN

IRAN
AFGHANISTAN

KUWAIT
BAHRAIN
QATAR
U.A.E.
SAUDI
ARABIA
OMAN

ERITREA
YEMEN

DJIBOUTI

PAKISTAN

CHINA

NORTH
KOREA
JAPAN

SOUTH
KOREA

NEPAL
BHUTAN

BANGLADESH

INDIA
MYANMAR
(BURMA)
LAOS

THAILAND
VIETNAM

CAMBODIA

SRI
LANKA

MALDIVES

Socotra
(Yemen)

EQUATOR

TAIWAN

PACIFIC
OCEAN

Northern
Mariana
Islands
(U.S.)

Guam
(U.S.)

PHILIPPINES

PALAU

MARSHALL
ISLANDS

FEDERATED STATES
OF MICRONESIA

KIRIBATI

NAURU

BRUNEI
MALAYSIA
SINGAPORE

INDONESIA

PAPUA
NEW GUINEA

TIMOR-LESTE

TUVALU

SOLOMON
ISLANDS

INDIAN

OCEAN

VANUATU

New Caledonia
(France)

FIJI

AUSTRALIA

NEW
ZEALAND

Kerguelen
Islands
(France)

Auckland Islands
(N.Z.)

SOUTHERN OCEAN

ANTARCTICA

N
W E
S

0   2000 miles

0   3000 kilometers

NORTH AMERICA

North America is shaped like a triangle. It is wide in the north. In the south, it becomes a strip of land only 30 miles (48 km) wide at its narrowest point. There, the Panama Canal connects the Atlantic and Pacific Oceans. The warm islands in the Caribbean Sea are part of North America. So is icy Greenland in the far north. The seven countries between Mexico and South America make up a region commonly called Central America. It connects the rest of North America to South America.

A brown bear, known as a grizzly bear in North America, walks through a meadow.

The Brooklyn Bridge crosses the East River, connecting Brooklyn and Manhattan in New York, U.S.A.

A male moose steps out of a lake in Glacier National Park, Montana, U.S.A. Moose are strong swimmers.

LAND REGIONS The Rocky Mountains stretch through western North America into Mexico, where the mountains are called the Sierra Madre Oriental. Older, lower mountains called the Appalachians are in the east. Grassy plains lie between these two mountain chains.

WATER Together, the Mississippi and its tributary the Missouri make up the continent's longest river. The Great Lakes are the world's largest group of freshwater lakes.

CLIMATE The far north is icy cold. Temperatures get warmer as you move south. Deserts cover dry areas in the southwest, but much of Central America is wet and hot.

PLANTS Large forests grow where rain or snow is plentiful. Grasslands cover areas with less precipitation.

ANIMALS The continent has a wide variety of animals: everything from bears, moose, and wolves to monkeys and colorful parrots.

North America is famous for its deciduous forests. Leaves turn fiery colors each fall before they drop from the trees.

The Pacific coast of Costa Rica is lined with beautiful beaches of white sands, clear waters, and bright green plants.

The Mitten Buttes are rock formations created by uplifting, weathering, and erosion in the desert habitat of southwestern North America.

American alligators have "armor" on their backs called scutes. Alligators live in freshwater habitats in the eastern parts of the United States.

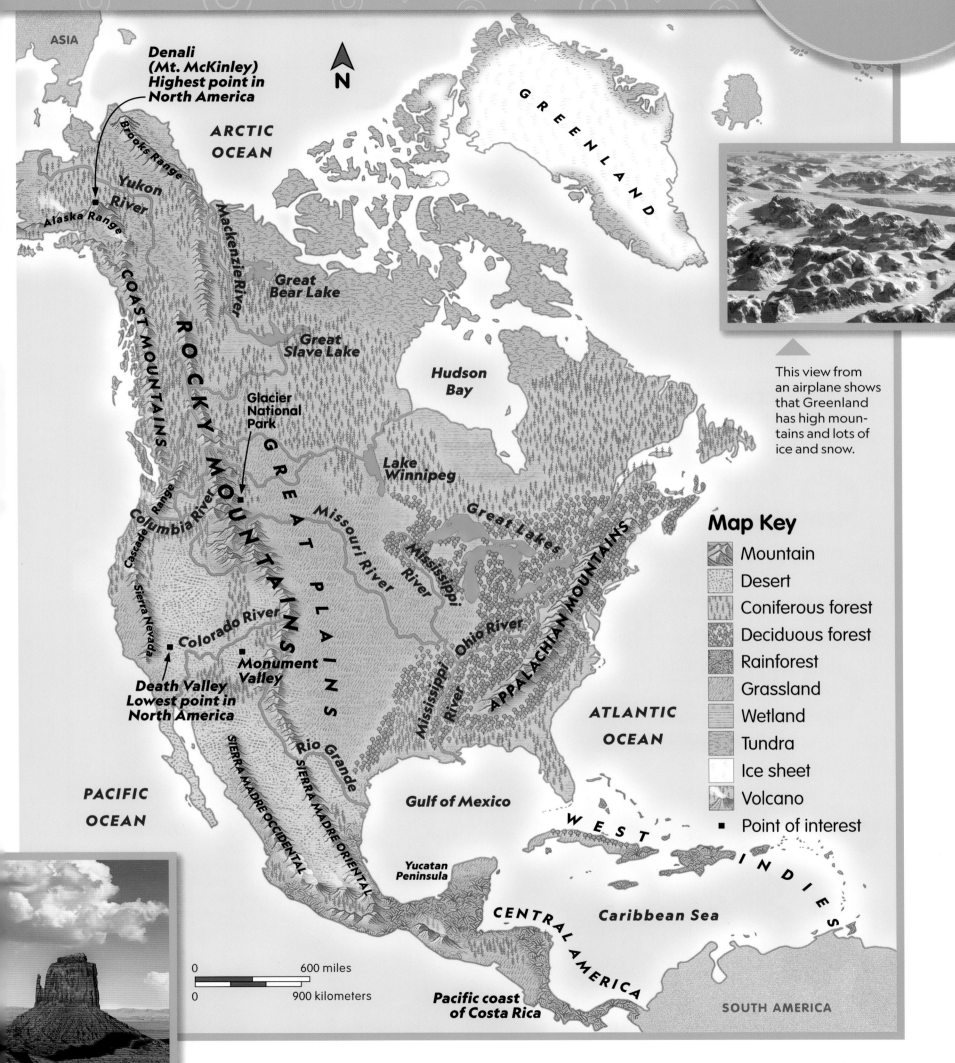

ASIA

Denali
(Mt. McKinley)
Highest point in
North America

N

ARCTIC
OCEAN

G R E E N L A N D

Brooks Range

Yukon
River

Alaska Range

Mackenzie River

COAST MOUNTAINS

R O C K Y   M O U N T A I N S

Great
Bear Lake

Great
Slave Lake

Hudson
Bay

Glacier
National
Park

Columbia River

Cascade Range

Colorado River

Sierra Nevada

Death Valley
Lowest point in
North America

Colorado River

Monument
Valley

G R E A T   P L A I N S

Missouri River

Mississippi
River

Lake
Winnipeg

Great Lakes

Mississippi
River

Ohio River

APPALACHIAN MOUNTAINS

ATLANTIC
OCEAN

This view from
an airplane shows
that Greenland
has high moun-
tains and lots of
ice and snow.

Map Key

Mountain

Desert

Coniferous forest

Deciduous forest

Rainforest

Grassland

Wetland

Tundra

Ice sheet

Volcano

■ Point of interest

PACIFIC
OCEAN

SIERRA MADRE OCCIDENTAL

SIERRA MADRE ORIENTAL

Rio Grande

Gulf of Mexico

Yucatan
Peninsula

W E S T   I N D I E S

Caribbean Sea

C E N T R A L   A M E R I C A

0   600 miles

0   900 kilometers

Pacific coast
of Costa Rica

SOUTH AMERICA

Snowboarding and skiing are popular sports in mountain areas.

This farmer is harvesting wheat on a big farm in Canada. Canada and the United States are among the world's biggest wheat producers.

COUNTRIES Canada, the United States, Mexico, and the countries of Central America and the West Indies make up North America.

CITIES Mexico City is the most populous city in North America, followed by the U.S. cities of New York and Los Angeles. Santo Domingo, in the Dominican Republic, is the most populous city in the West Indies.

PEOPLE The ancestors of most people in North America came from Europe. Many other people trace their roots to Africa and Asia. Various groups of Native Americans live throughout the continent.

LANGUAGES English and Spanish are the main languages. A large number of people in Canada and Haiti speak French. There are also many Native American languages.

The Palacio de Bellas Artes is one of the most well-known monuments in Mexico City.

These red berries hold coffee beans. Many farmers in Guatemala make a living growing coffee.

These children from the country of Trinidad and Tobago in the West Indies are dressed up to celebrate a festival called Carnival.

Cliff Palace, part of Mesa Verde National Park, in Colorado, U.S.A., was built long ago by Native Americans. It is the largest cliff dwelling in North America.

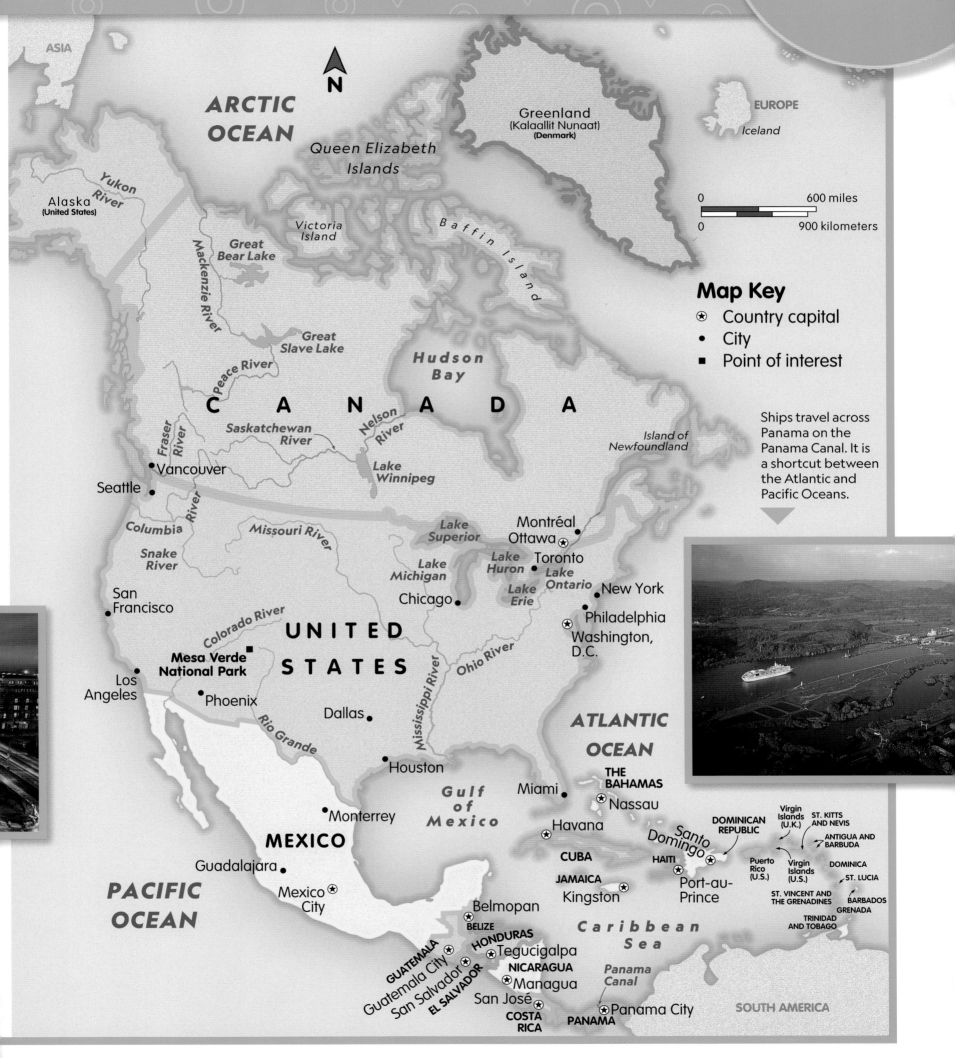

ASIA

ARCTIC OCEAN

Queen Elizabeth Islands

Greenland
(Kalaallit Nunaat)
(Denmark)

EUROPE

Iceland

Yukon River

Alaska
(United States)

Victoria Island

B a f f i n   I s l a n d

Great Bear Lake

Mackenzie River

Great Slave Lake

Peace River

Hudson Bay

0   600 miles

0   900 kilometers

Map Key

⊛ Country capital

• City

■ Point of interest

C A N A D A

Fraser River

Saskatchewan River

Nelson River

Island of Newfoundland

Lake Winnipeg

Ships travel across Panama on the Panama Canal. It is a shortcut between the Atlantic and Pacific Oceans.

Vancouver

Seattle

Columbia

River

Snake River

Missouri River

Lake Superior

Lake Michigan

Lake Huron

Lake Ontario

Lake Erie

Montréal

Ottawa ⊛

Toronto

New York

San Francisco

Chicago

U N I T E D

S T A T E S

Colorado River

Mississippi River

Ohio River

Philadelphia

Washington, D.C. ⊛

■ Mesa Verde National Park

Los Angeles

Phoenix

Dallas

Rio Grande

ATLANTIC OCEAN

Houston

Miami

THE BAHAMAS

Nassau ⊛

G u l f o f M e x i c o

Monterrey

MEXICO

Havana ⊛

Santo Domingo ⊛

DOMINICAN REPUBLIC

Virgin Islands (U.K.)

ST. KITTS AND NEVIS

ANTIGUA AND BARBUDA

CUBA

HAITI

Puerto Rico (U.S.)

Virgin Islands (U.S.)

DOMINICA

Guadalajara

JAMAICA

Kingston ⊛

Port-au-Prince

ST. LUCIA

PACIFIC OCEAN

Mexico City ⊛

Port-au-Prince

ST. VINCENT AND THE GRENADINES

BARBADOS

GRENADA

TRINIDAD AND TOBAGO

Belmopan ⊛

BELIZE

C a r i b b e a n

S e a

GUATEMALA

Guatemala City ⊛

HONDURAS

Tegucigalpa ⊛

San Salvador ⊛

NICARAGUA

Panama Canal

EL SALVADOR

Managua ⊛

San José ⊛

COSTA RICA

Panama City ⊛

PANAMA

SOUTH AMERICA

The Great Lakes are the largest freshwater lakes on the continent. This is Lake Huron. Can you name the other four?

STATES The United States is made up of 50 states. Alaska and Hawai'i are separated from the rest of the country. To let you see them close up, they are shown near the bottom of the map. Use the small globe above to see their real locations.

CITIES Washington, D.C., is the country's capital. Each state also has a capital city. Of all the cities, New York City has the most people.

PEOPLE People from almost every country in the world live in the United States. Most live and work in and around cities.

LANGUAGES English is the main language, followed by Spanish.

Lacrosse is a Native American game played widely across the United States and Canada. Here a young player shouts with joy during a game.

A parade in Kansas to celebrate Día de los Muertos, the Day of the Dead, honors loved ones who have passed away.

Yellowstone National Park, located mostly in Wyoming, was the first national park created in the world.

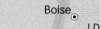

Seattle
Olympia
Columbia River
WASHINGTON
Portland
Salem
OREGON
Boise
ID

Carson City
Sacramento
San Francisco
NEVADA
San Jose
CALIFORNIA
Las Vegas
Los Angeles
San Diego
AR

PACIFIC OCEAN

ALASKA
Juneau

| 0 | 400 miles |
| 0 | 600 kilometers |

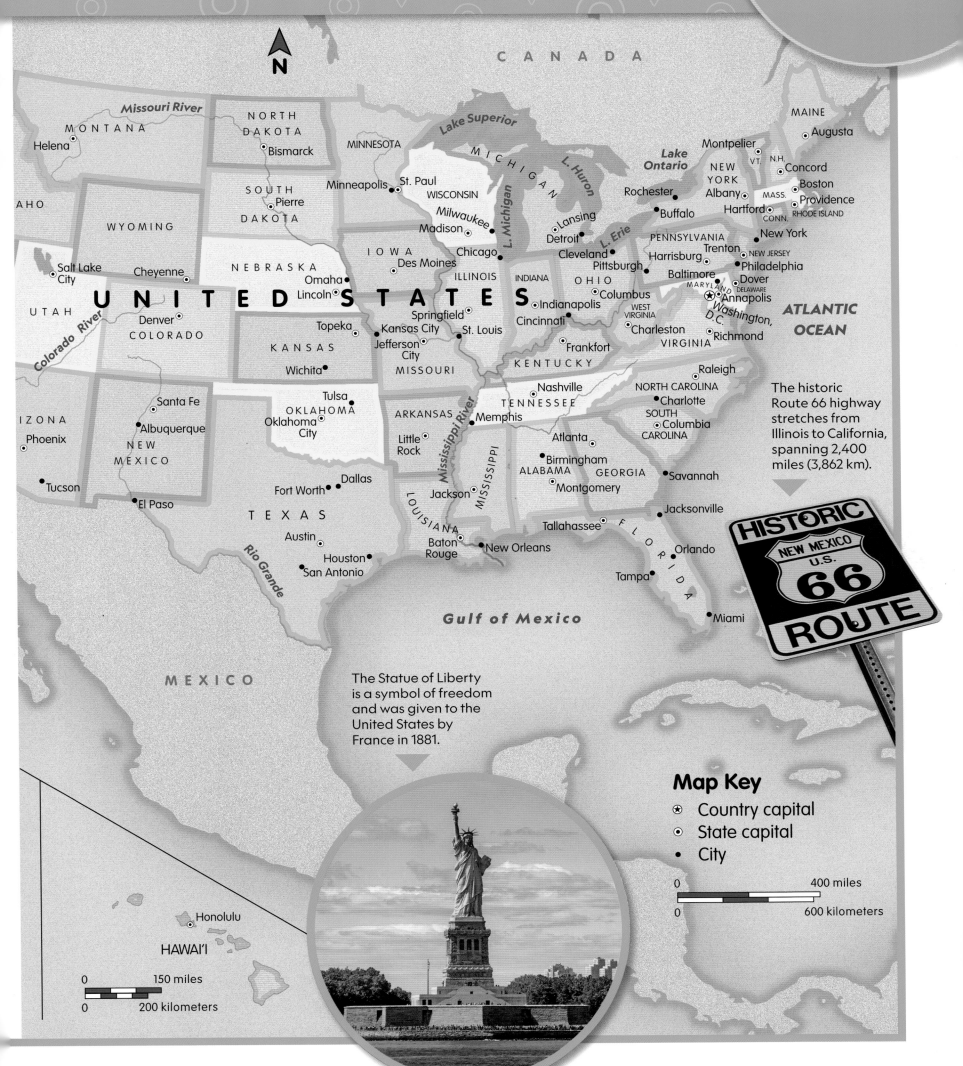

N

CANADA

MONTANA
Helena

NORTH DAKOTA
Bismarck

MINNESOTA

Lake Superior

MICHIGAN

L. Huron

MAINE
Augusta

Montpelier
NEW YORK
VT. N.H. Concord
Albany Boston
Hartford MASS. Providence
CONN. RHODE ISLAND

IAHO

SOUTH DAKOTA
Pierre

WYOMING

St. Paul
Minneapolis
WISCONSIN
Milwaukee
Madison

Lansing
Detroit

L. Michigan

Lake Ontario
Rochester
Buffalo

L. Erie

PENNSYLVANIA
Cleveland Harrisburg Trenton NEW JERSEY
Pittsburgh Baltimore Philadelphia
MARYLAND Dover DELAWARE
Annapolis
Washington, D.C.
ATLANTIC OCEAN

Salt Lake City
Cheyenne

NEBRASKA
Omaha
Lincoln

IOWA
Des Moines

ILLINOIS
Chicago

INDIANA

OHIO
Columbus
Indianapolis
WEST VIRGINIA
Charleston

UTAH

Colorado River

Denver
COLORADO

Topeka
Kansas City
Jefferson City

KANSAS

Springfield
St. Louis

Cincinnati

Frankfort

Richmond
VIRGINIA

UNITED STATES

Wichita

MISSOURI

KENTUCKY

Nashville

Raleigh
NORTH CAROLINA
Charlotte
SOUTH CAROLINA
Columbia

IZONA

Santa Fe
Albuquerque
NEW MEXICO
Phoenix

Tulsa
OKLAHOMA
Oklahoma City

ARKANSAS
Little Rock

Memphis

TENNESSEE

The historic Route 66 highway stretches from Illinois to California, spanning 2,400 miles (3,862 km).

Tucson

El Paso

Fort Worth Dallas

Mississippi River

MISSISSIPPI

Atlanta

Birmingham
ALABAMA
Montgomery

GEORGIA

Savannah

TEXAS

Austin

Rio Grande

Houston
San Antonio

LOUISIANA
Jackson
Baton Rouge New Orleans

Tallahassee

FLORIDA

Jacksonville

Orlando

Tampa

Miami

HISTORIC
NEW MEXICO
U.S.
66
ROUTE

Gulf of Mexico

MEXICO

The Statue of Liberty is a symbol of freedom and was given to the United States by France in 1881.

Map Key
⊛ Country capital
◉ State capital
• City

0   400 miles
0   600 kilometers

Honolulu

HAWAI'I

0   150 miles
0   200 kilometers

CANADA

This artwork in Vancouver, Canada, has traditional designs of the Coast Salish culture, which show the connection between people and nature.

PROVINCES Canada is divided into 10 provinces and three territories. Most people live in Ontario and Quebec.

CITIES Ottawa is Canada's capital. Toronto, Montréal, and Vancouver are among its largest cities and ports.

PEOPLE Canada has fewer people than the U.S. state of California. Most Canadians live within 100 miles (160 km) of the country's southern border. There are three groups of Indigenous people in Canada: First Nations, Inuit, and Metis.

LANGUAGES Canada's street signs are often in two languages—English and French, the main languages. Most French-speaking Canadians live in Quebec.

Alaska (U.S.)

YUKON

Mackenzie River

Yukon River

⊙ Whitehorse

BRITISH

Peace

COLUMBIA

Fraser River

Vancouver Island

Victoria ⊙

• Vancouver

Québec is the only walled city in North America north of Mexico.

During Canada's long, cold winters, ice hockey is a popular sport. The Hockey Hall of Fame is in Toronto, Ontario.

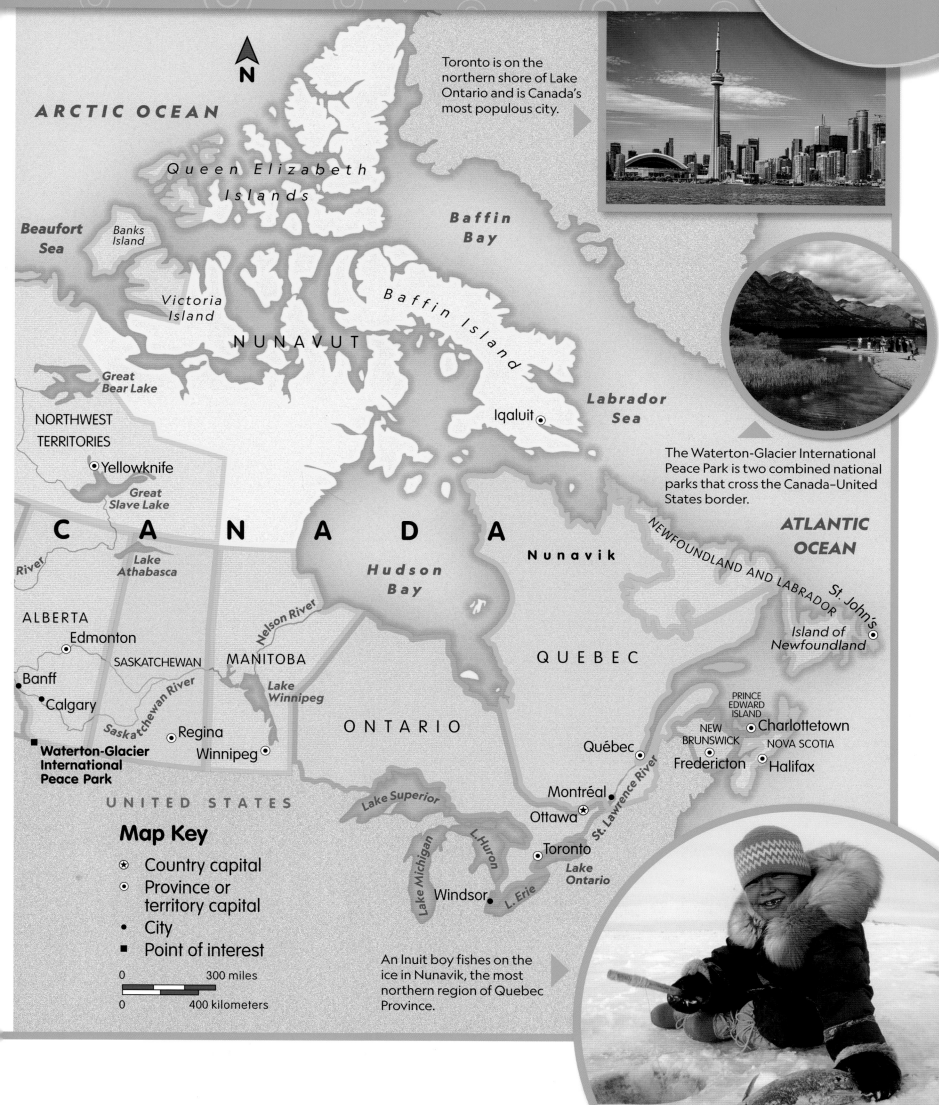

Toronto is on the northern shore of Lake Ontario and is Canada's most populous city.

The Waterton-Glacier International Peace Park is two combined national parks that cross the Canada–United States border.

ARCTIC OCEAN

Queen Elizabeth Islands

Beaufort Sea

Banks Island

Baffin Bay

Victoria Island

Baffin Island

NUNAVUT

Great Bear Lake

Labrador Sea

NORTHWEST TERRITORIES

Iqaluit ⊙

⊙ Yellowknife

Great Slave Lake

C A N A D A

River

Lake Athabasca

Nunavik

Hudson Bay

NEWFOUNDLAND AND LABRADOR

ATLANTIC OCEAN

ALBERTA

Edmonton ⊙

SASKATCHEWAN

MANITOBA

Nelson River

Q U E B E C

St. John's ⊙

Island of Newfoundland

Banff •

• Calgary

Saskatchewan River

Lake Winnipeg

■ **Waterton-Glacier International Peace Park**

⊙ Regina

Winnipeg ⊙

O N T A R I O

PRINCE EDWARD ISLAND

⊙ Charlottetown

Québec ⊙

NEW BRUNSWICK

NOVA SCOTIA

Fredericton ⊙ ⊙ Halifax

U N I T E D   S T A T E S

Lake Superior

Montréal •

Ottawa ⊛

St. Lawrence River

Map Key

⊛ Country capital

⊙ Province or territory capital

• City

■ Point of interest

Lake Michigan

L. Huron

Toronto ⊙

Lake Ontario

Windsor •

L. Erie

0	300 miles
0	400 kilometers

An Inuit boy fishes on the ice in Nunavik, the most northern region of Quebec Province.

SOUTH AMERICA

South America is a land of many amazing things, including the world's biggest rainforest (the Amazon) and one of its driest deserts (the Atacama). It has mysterious ruins and crowded modern cities. In the mountains, llamas carry heavy loads. On the grasslands, cowboys called gauchos herd cattle. Foods such as potatoes and tomatoes are native to South America.

The strawberry poison dart frog can range in color from this vivid orange to yellow, white, or even a brilliant blue.

Vinicunca, or Rainbow Mountain, in the Peruvian Andes gets its beautiful colors from the minerals that make up the rock and soil on the mountain.

Llamas are native to the Andes and are used to carry heavy loads for people.

LAND REGIONS Snowcapped mountains called the Andes run along the west coast. Rainforests and grasslands cover much of the rest of the continent. The continent's driest desert lies between the Andes and the Pacific Ocean.

WATER The Amazon River carries more water than any other river in the world. More than 1,000 streams and rivers flow into it. Lake Titicaca is the continent's largest lake.

CLIMATE Much of South America is warm all year. The coldest places are in the Andes and at the continent's southern tip. Each year more than 80 inches (200 cm) of rain falls in the rainforests.

PLANTS The Amazon rainforest has more kinds of plants than any other place in the world. In the south, grasslands feed large herds of cattle and sheep.

ANIMALS Colorful toucans, noisy howler monkeys, and giant snakes live in the rainforests. Sure-footed llamas, huge birds called condors, and guinea pigs live in the Andes. The flightless rhea, which looks like an ostrich, roams the wide southern grasslands.

Parts of the Atacama Desert, in northern Chile, have not had rainfall in decades.

A young black caiman sits on a royal water lily pad, the world's largest water lily, in Guyana.

These big, colorful macaws live in the rainforest. They are a type of parrot.

Butterflies drink the salty tears of a yellow-spotted Amazon River turtle in the Amazon Basin.

NORTH AMERICA

Lake Maracaibo

Orinoco River

Angel Falls
Tallest waterfall in the world

Largest water lilies in the world

N

A M A Z O N

Negro River

Amazon River

Amazon River

EQUATOR

EQUATOR

B A S I N

PACIFIC

OCEAN

Lake Titicaca

Driest place in the world

Atacama Desert

A N D E S

Paraguay River

Paraná River

Iguazú Falls

Paraná River

ATLANTIC

OCEAN

Cerro Aconcagua
Highest point in South America

Rio de la Plata

Map Key

Mountain

Desert

Rainforest

Grassland

Wetland

Volcano

■ Point of interest

" Waterfall

Laguna del Carbón
Lowest point in South America

Strait of Magellan

Falkland Islands

0   600 miles

0   900 kilometers

Many religious festivals take place all over South America. Here, a girl is dancing as she celebrates a Catholic fiesta.

This statue was carved from stone during the Tiwanaku civilization. These people lived long ago near Lake Titicaca in Bolivia.

COUNTRIES South America has just 12 countries—French Guiana is not a country because it belongs to France. All but two of these countries border an ocean. Can you find these two landlocked countries on the map?

CITIES Most of the largest cities are near the oceans. São Paulo, in Brazil, is South America's most populous city. Bolivia has two capital cities: La Paz and Sucre.

PEOPLE The earliest people came from the north long ago. Colonists came from Europe, especially from Spain and Portugal. They brought enslaved people from Africa to work in the fields. Most people in South America are descendants of these three groups.

LANGUAGES Spanish and Portuguese are the continent's main languages. Native people speak Quechua or other native languages.

A Peruvian woman weaves pallay, or designs in the weavings, that are known for their bright patterns.

These unpolished stones are emeralds. Colombia is the top producer of these gems.

Soccer is the most popular sport in South America. This player from Brazil is focused on scoring a goal.

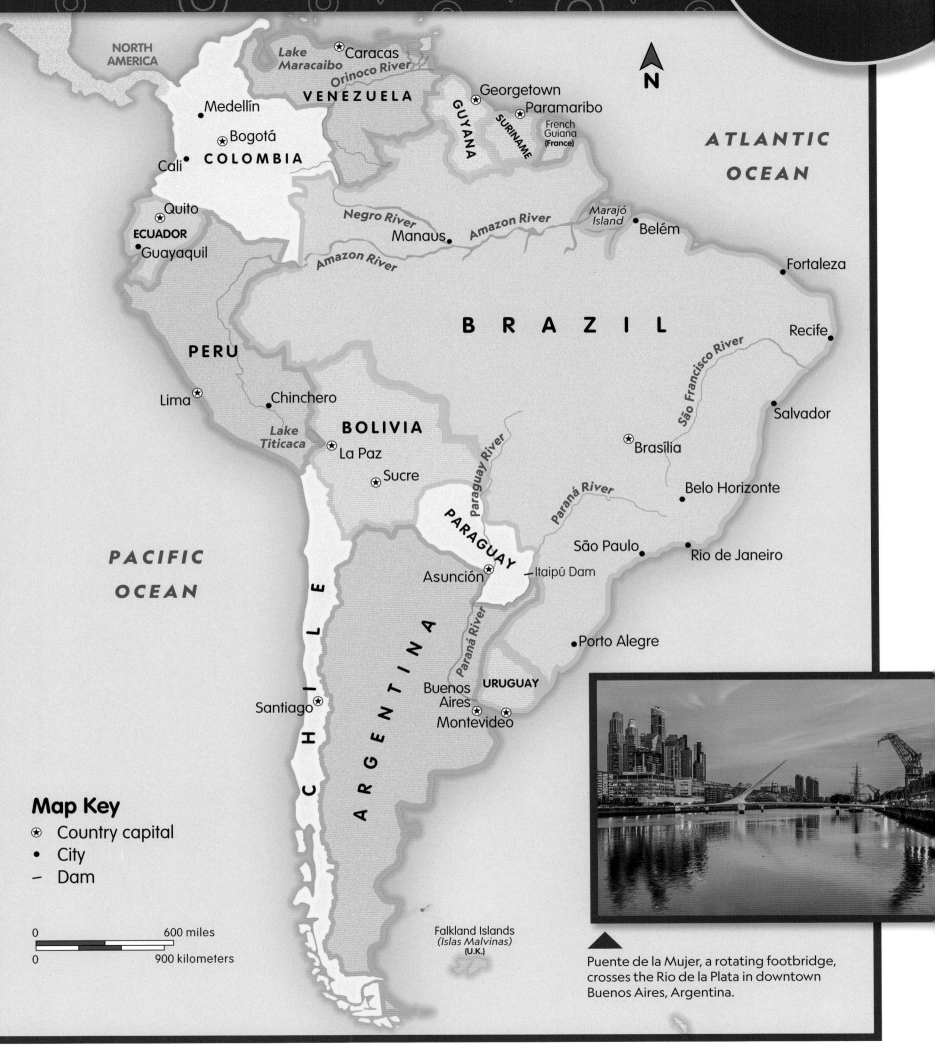

NORTH AMERICA

Lake Maracaibo

⊛ Caracas

Orinoco River

VENEZUELA

Medellín

⊛ Bogotá

COLOMBIA

Cali

Georgetown

Paramaribo

GUYANA

SURINAME

French Guiana (France)

ATLANTIC OCEAN

N

Quito ⊛

ECUADOR

Guayaquil

Negro River

Amazon River

Manaus

Amazon River

Marajó Island

Belém

Fortaleza

B R A Z I L

PERU

Lima ⊛

Chinchero

São Francisco River

Recife

Salvador

Lake Titicaca

BOLIVIA

⊛ La Paz

Paraguay River

Brasília ⊛

PACIFIC OCEAN

⊛ Sucre

Paraná River

Belo Horizonte

PARAGUAY

São Paulo

Rio de Janeiro

Asunción ⊛

—Itaipú Dam

Paraná River

Porto Alegre

C H I L E

A R G E N T I N A

URUGUAY

Buenos Aires

Santiago ⊛

Montevideo

Map Key

⊛ Country capital

• City

— Dam

| 0 | | 600 miles |
| 0 | | 900 kilometers |

Falkland Islands (Islas Malvinas) (U.K.)

Puente de la Mujer, a rotating footbridge, crosses the Rio de la Plata in downtown Buenos Aires, Argentina.

EUROPE

T ravel through the countryside in Europe and you're likely to see castles, cuckoo clocks, and cobblestone streets. But Europe is also one of the most modern continents. You can ride one of the world's fastest trains through a tunnel beneath the English Channel, watch sports cars being made in Italy, and visit famous landmarks, such as the Eiffel Tower, in Paris. On a map, Europe may look as if it is part of Asia, but it is considered to be a separate continent.

Eurasian lynx can be found in woody or mountainous areas from western Europe through Russia and into Central Asia.

The reconstructed Stari Most, or the Old Bridge of Mostar, crosses the Neretva River in Bosnia and Herzegovina.

Iceland

Giant's Causeway in Northern Ireland was formed between 50 and 60 million years ago when lava leaked from cracks in the earth and cooled.

LAND REGIONS Europe's most obvious feature is its long coastline, cut with bays and peninsulas of every size. The Alps are high mountains that form a chain across a large part of southern Europe.

WATER Several large rivers flow across Europe. Some of the most important are the Danube, Rhine, and Volga.

CLIMATE Warm winds from the Atlantic Ocean help give much of Europe a mild, rainy climate. This climate makes parts of Europe good for farming.

PLANTS Europe's largest forests are in the north. Cork and olive trees grow near the Mediterranean Sea.

ANIMALS Reindeer are common in the far north. Many kinds of goatlike animals live in the Alps. Robins, nightingales, and sparrows are among Europe's native birds.

ATLANTIC OCEAN

Giant's Causeway

Ireland

Great Britain

People often try to climb the Matterhorn. It is one of the highest peaks in the Alps.

PYRENEES

IBERIAN PENINSULA

A fjord, like this one in Norway, is a valley that was carved by a glacier and then flooded with seawater.

M e

AFRICA

The alpine newt is a cold-adapted amphibian that mostly lives in the mountains of central Europe.

N

Norwegian Sea

SCANDINAVIAN PENINSULA

Sogn og Fjordane, Naeroyfjord

Baltic Sea

North Sea

NORTHERN EUROPEAN PLAIN

Rhine River

URAL MTS.

ASIA

Volga River

EUROPE-ASIA BOUNDARY

Caspian Sea Lowest point in Europe

CARPATHIAN MTS.

THE STEPPES

El'brus Highest point in Europe

Rhône River

A L P S

← Matterhorn

Danube River

BALKAN MTS.

CAUCASUS MTS.

APENNINES

Black Sea

Caspian Sea

ASIA

Sicily

→ **Mount Etna**

M e d i t e r r a n e a n   S e a

Crete   **Cyprus**

Map Key

- Mountain
- Desert
- Coniferous forest
- Deciduous forest
- Grassland
- Wetland
- Tundra
- Volcano
- ■ Point of interest
- — Europe-Asia boundary

Spending most of its time at sea, the Atlantic puffin will nest on rocky sea cliffs with low-growing plants.

0   600 miles

0   900 kilometers

Dressed for the Fallas festival that celebrates the arrival of spring, these girls honor the history of the Silk Roads in Spain.

ICELAND
Reykjavík

Faroe Islands (Denmark)

ATLANTIC OCEAN

Orkney Islands

Cars are one of Europe's most valuable exports.

SCOTLAND

IRELAND (ÉIRE)
Dublin

UNITED KINGDOM

London

English Channel

Paris

FRA

Bordeaux

PORTUGAL

ANDORRA

Madrid

Lisbon   SPAIN

Sevilla

Balearic Islands (Spain)

Gibraltar (U.K.)

COUNTRIES Europe has 46 countries. Even though most of Russia is in Asia (see pages 42–43), it is usually counted as part of Europe because most of its people live there. Vatican City, Europe's smallest country, lies within the city of Rome, Italy. There are five island countries: Iceland, the United Kingdom, Ireland, Malta, and Cyprus.

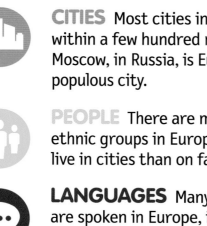

CITIES Most cities in Europe are within a few hundred miles of the sea. Moscow, in Russia, is Europe's most populous city.

PEOPLE There are many different ethnic groups in Europe. More people live in cities than on farms.

LANGUAGES Many different languages are spoken in Europe, including English, French, German, and Russian.

The euro is currently the official money of 19 member countries of the European Union (see page 61).

The Colosseum lights up as the sun begins to set in Rome, Italy. This amphitheater was built by the Roman Empire almost 2,000 years ago.

The countries that surround the Mediterranean Sea are known for their mild weather, beautiful beaches, and stunning villages, like this one on the island of Malta.

Map Key
⊛ Country capital
• City

0 — 600 miles
0 — 900 kilometers

Norwegian Sea

ASIA

EUROPE-ASIA BOUNDARY

N

Shetland Islands

NORWAY

SWEDEN

FINLAND

Helsinki ⊛
• St. Petersburg

Oslo ⊛
Stockholm ⊛
⊛ Tallinn
ESTONIA

R U S S I A

North Sea

Baltic Sea

Riga ⊛
LATVIA

⊛ Moscow

DENMARK
Copenhagen ⊛

LITHUANIA

Kaliningrad (Russia)

⊛ Vilnius

⊛ Minsk
BELARUS

Volga River

KAZAKHSTAN

The Hague
⊛ Amsterdam
NETHERLANDS
• Hamburg
Berlin ⊛
Warsaw ⊛

Brussels ⊛
BELGIUM
LUXEMBOURG

GERMANY

Rhine River

POLAND

• Kraków

⊛ Kyiv

Volgograd •

N C E

Prague ⊛
CZECHIA (CZECH REPUBLIC)

Danube River

U K R A I N E

SLOVAKIA
Vienna ⊛ ⊛ Bratislava
AUSTRIA

⊛ Budapest
HUNGARY

MOLDOVA
Chisinau ⊛

Caspian Sea

Bern ⊛
SWITZERLAND
LIECHTENSTEIN

SLOVENIA
Ljubljana ⊛ ⊛ Zagreb
CROATIA

ROMANIA

Crimea

GEORGIA
Tbilisi ⊛

Baku ⊛

Rhône R.

SAN MARINO

Belgrade ⊛

Bucharest ⊛

Danube River

Black Sea

AZERBAIJAN

MONACO

BOSNIA AND HERZEGOVINA
Sarajevo ⊛
SERBIA

NOTE: The countries of Turkey, Georgia, Azerbaijan, Kazakhstan, and Russia are in both Europe and Asia.

Corsica (France)

ITALY

MONTENEGRO
Podgorica ⊛

KOSOVO
⊛ Pristina

BULGARIA
⊛ Sofia

VATICAN CITY
Rome ⊛

Skopje ⊛
NORTH MACEDONIA

ASIA

Sardinia (Italy)

• Naples

Tirana ⊛
ALBANIA

GREECE

Istanbul •

⊛ Ankara

T U R K E Y

Sicily

Mediterranean Sea

⊛ Athens

Valletta ⊛
MALTA

Crete

⊛ Nicosia
CYPRUS

AFRICA

St. Basil's is a famous Russian Orthodox church. It is in Moscow, Russia's capital city.

▶

ASIA

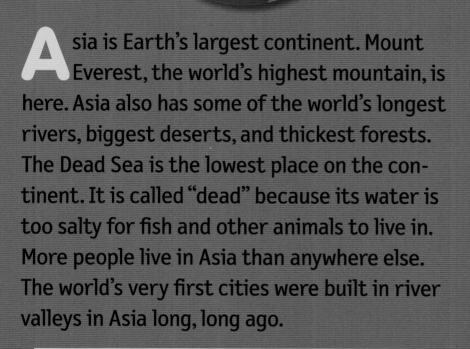

Asia is Earth's largest continent. Mount Everest, the world's highest mountain, is here. Asia also has some of the world's longest rivers, biggest deserts, and thickest forests. The Dead Sea is the lowest place on the continent. It is called "dead" because its water is too salty for fish and other animals to live in. More people live in Asia than anywhere else. The world's very first cities were built in river valleys in Asia long, long ago.

Covered in scales to protect against predators, the Indian pangolin lives all over southern Asia.

Shanghai, China, has the largest population of any city in China and is one of the world's largest seaports.

Mount Everest, in the Himalayan mountains, is 29,032 feet (8,849 m) high.

 LAND REGIONS Much of Asia is a rolling plain covered by grasslands, forests, and tundra. The Himalaya and other high mountains stretch across the south. Deserts cover much of southwestern and central Asia.

WATER Asia has huge rivers and lakes. The Yangtze is the longest river. The Caspian Sea (partly in Europe) is the world's largest saltwater lake. Lake Baikal is the world's deepest lake.

 CLIMATE Northern Asia has long, cold winters and short, cool summers. Most of southern Asia is warm year-round with heavy summer rains.

PLANTS Areas of coniferous forest called taiga stretch across the north. The central grasslands are known as the steppes. Rainforests grow in the southeast.

 ANIMALS Tigers, giant pandas, and cobras live in the wild only in Asia.

Mediterranean Sea

Black Sea

CAUCASUS MTS.

Euphrates River

Tigris River

Dead Sea
Lowest point
in Asia

Persian Gulf

AFRICA

ARABIAN PENINSULA

EQUATOR

A dromedary, or one-hump, camel walks across the vast desert of the Arabian Peninsula. Camels can carry heavy loads across the desert, are a source of food, and provide hair for weaving cloth.

The Mekong River Delta, where the Mekong River meets the South China Sea, is an important source of water and food for people in Southeast Asia.

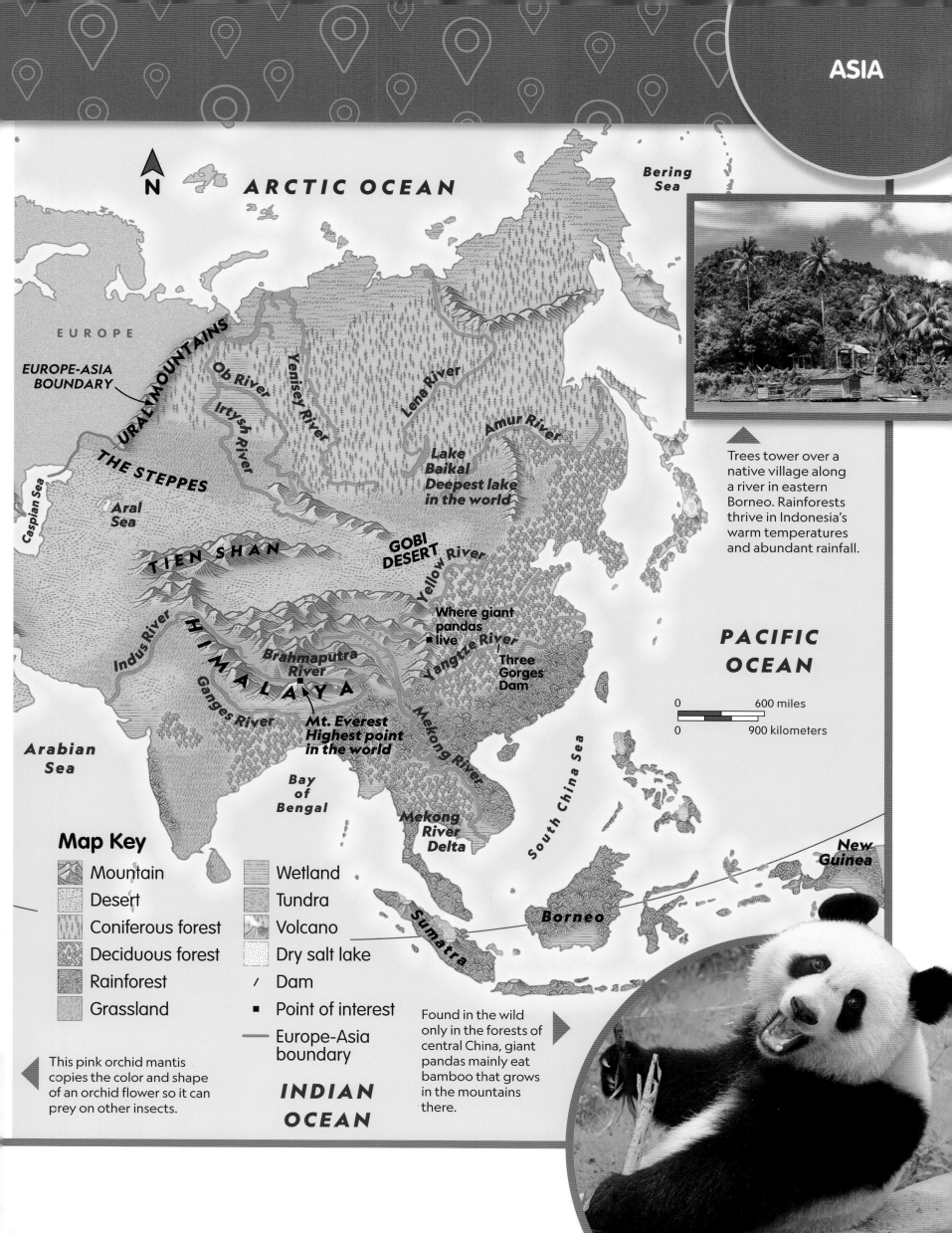

N

ARCTIC OCEAN

Bering Sea

EUROPE

EUROPE-ASIA BOUNDARY

URAL MOUNTAINS

THE STEPPES

Ob River

Yenisey River

Irtysh River

Lena River

Amur River

Aral Sea

Caspian Sea

Lake Baikal
Deepest lake in the world

TIEN SHAN

GOBI DESERT

Yellow River

Where giant pandas live

Indus River

H I M A L A Y A

Brahmaputra River

Ganges River

Yangtze River

Three Gorges Dam

**Mt. Everest
Highest point in the world**

Mekong River

Arabian Sea

Bay of Bengal

Mekong River Delta

South China Sea

PACIFIC OCEAN

Trees tower over a native village along a river in eastern Borneo. Rainforests thrive in Indonesia's warm temperatures and abundant rainfall.

0 — 600 miles
0 — 900 kilometers

New Guinea

Borneo

Sumatra

Map Key

- Mountain
- Desert
- Coniferous forest
- Deciduous forest
- Rainforest
- Grassland
- Wetland
- Tundra
- Volcano
- Dry salt lake
- ⁄ Dam
- ▪ Point of interest
- — Europe-Asia boundary

Found in the wild only in the forests of central China, giant pandas mainly eat bamboo that grows in the mountains there.

This pink orchid mantis copies the color and shape of an orchid flower so it can prey on other insects.

INDIAN OCEAN

These are the Petronas Towers in Kuala Lumpur, Malaysia. They are the tallest twin buildings in the world.

COUNTRIES Asia has 46 countries. China is the largest country with boundaries entirely in Asia. Russia takes up the most area, but it is counted as part of Europe (see pages 36–37). Indonesia is Asia's largest island country.

CITIES Much of Asia is too high, too dry, or too cold for people to live in. Most cities are near the coast or along busy rivers. Tokyo, in Japan, is the most populous city.

PEOPLE Asia has more people than any other continent. Each ethnic group has its own language, customs, and appearance. Many people are farmers, but others work in high-tech industries.

LANGUAGES About 2,300 languages are spoken by the people of Asia—the most of any continent. Mandarin is the most widely spoken language in Asia.

EUROPE
RUSSIA
Baltic

NOTE: The countries of Russia, Kazakhstan, Azerbaijan, Georgia, and Turkey are in both Europe and Asia.

Black
Istanbul
Ankara ⊛
Sea
GEORGIA
TURKEY
Tbilisi ⊛
ARMENIA
LEBANON
Beirut ⊛ SYRIA Yerevan ⊛
Cairo ⊛ ISRAEL ⊛ Damascus
AZERBAIJAN
Jerusalem ⊛ ⊛ Amman
EGYPT
JORDAN
Baghdad ⊛ Tehran ⊛
IRAQ
I R
KUWAIT ⊛ Kuwait
SAUDI City
ARABIA BAHRAIN
NOTE: Egypt is in both Africa and Asia.
Riyadh ⊛ QATAR
Doha
Abu Dhabi ⊛
UNITED ARAB
EMIRATES
Sanaa ⊛
YEMEN **OMAN**
Mediterranean Sea
Persian Gulf

AFRICA

The Angkor Wat temple in Cambodia was originally dedicated to the Hindu god Vishnu. It is thought to be the largest religious structure in the world.

Holding a deepa, or clay lamp, this young girl celebrates Diwali, the festival of lights in India.

This boy in Shanghai, China, draws symbols used in writing the Chinese language. Each symbol stands for a word or an idea.

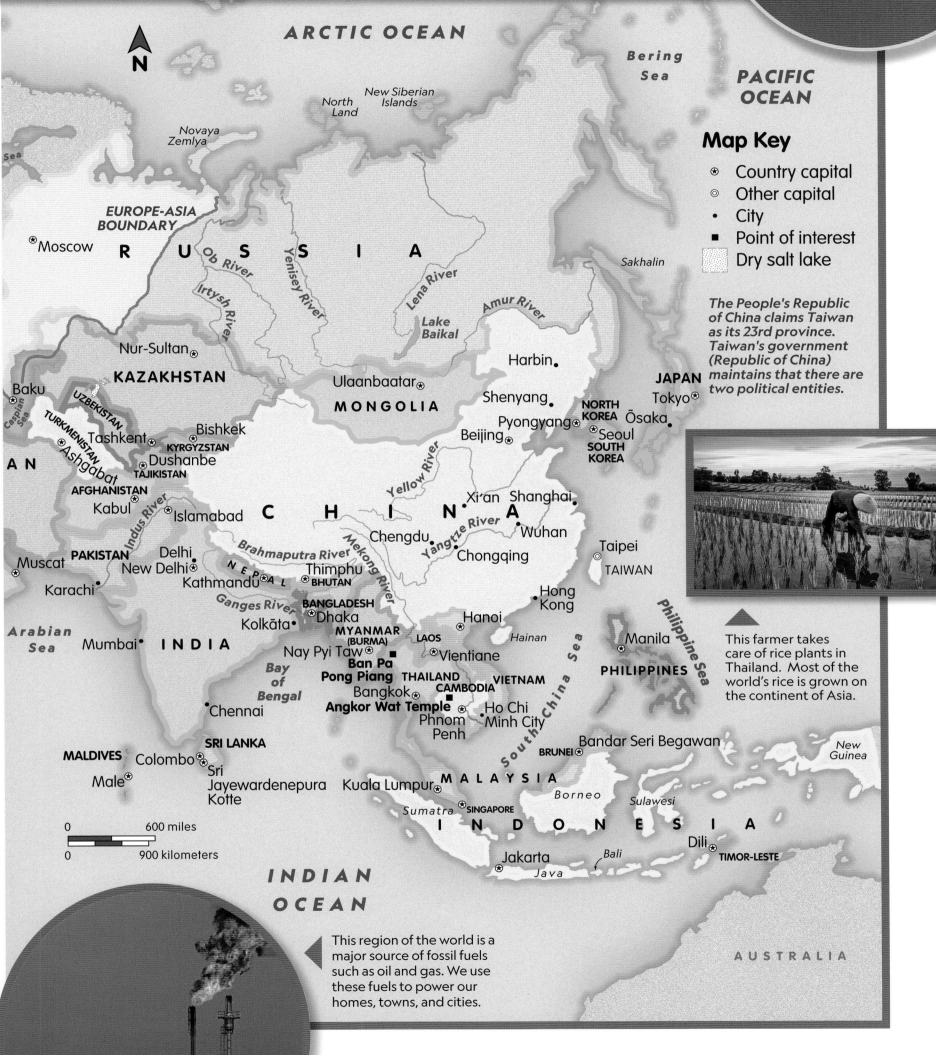

ARCTIC OCEAN

Bering Sea

PACIFIC OCEAN

New Siberian Islands

North Land

Novaya Zemlya

N

EUROPE-ASIA BOUNDARY

Sea

⊛Moscow

R U S S I A

Ob River

Irtysh River

Yenisey River

Lena River

Amur River

Lake Baikal

Sakhalin

Map Key

⊛ Country capital
◎ Other capital
· City
▪ Point of interest
▒ Dry salt lake

The People's Republic of China claims Taiwan as its 23rd province. Taiwan's government (Republic of China) maintains that there are two political entities.

Nur-Sultan⊛

KAZAKHSTAN

Ulaanbaatar⊛

M O N G O L I A

Harbin·

Shenyang·

JAPAN

Tokyo⊛

Baku⊛

UZBEKISTAN

TURKMENISTAN

Tashkent⊛

KYRGYZSTAN

Bishkek⊛

Beijing⊛

Pyongyang⊛

NORTH KOREA

⊛Seoul

Ōsaka·

Caspian Sea

Ashgabat⊛

Dushanbe⊛

TAJIKISTAN

SOUTH KOREA

A N

AFGHANISTAN

Kabul⊛

Islamabad⊛

Indus River

C H I N A

Xi'an·

Shanghai·

Chengdu·

Yangtze River

Wuhan·

Taipei◎

Muscat⊛

PAKISTAN

Delhi·

New Delhi⊛

Brahmaputra River

Mekong River

Chongqing·

TAIWAN

Karachi·

Thimphu⊛

N E P A L

BHUTAN

Kathmandu⊛

Yellow River

Hong Kong

Arabian Sea

Mumbai·

I N D I A

Ganges River

BANGLADESH

Dhaka⊛

Hanoi⊛

Hainan

Manila⊛

Philippine Sea

Kolkāta·

MYANMAR (BURMA)

LAOS

Nay Pyi Taw⊛

Ban Pa Pong Piang ▪

Vientiane◎

VIETNAM

PHILIPPINES

Bay of Bengal

THAILAND

Bangkok⊛

Angkor Wat Temple

CAMBODIA

Ho Chi Minh City·

South China Sea

·Chennai

Phnom Penh⊛

SRI LANKA

MALDIVES

Colombo◎

Sri Jayewardenepura Kotte⊛

Kuala Lumpur⊛

M A L A Y S I A

Borneo

Sulawesi

Bandar Seri Begawan⊛

New Guinea

Male⊛

BRUNEI

0 — 600 miles
0 — 900 kilometers

Sumatra

SINGAPORE⊛

I N D O N E S I A

Dili⊛

TIMOR-LESTE

Jakarta⊛

Bali

Java

I N D I A N

O C E A N

This farmer takes care of rice plants in Thailand. Most of the world's rice is grown on the continent of Asia.

This region of the world is a major source of fossil fuels such as oil and gas. We use these fuels to power our homes, towns, and cities.

A U S T R A L I A

AFRICA

Elephants, lions, gorillas, hippopotamuses, giraffes, and zebras are among the amazing animals you can see in Africa's parks, plains, forests, and mountains. You can also visit a busy, modern city such as Nairobi, in Kenya, and shop in colorful outdoor markets. You can even take a sailboat ride past ancient temples along the Nile and climb some of the world's highest sand dunes in Earth's biggest hot desert—the Sahara.

As the fastest mammal on land, a cheetah can reach a speed of 45 miles an hour (72 km/h) in only 2.5 seconds!

Mosi-oa-Tunya, or Victoria Falls, is one of the world's largest waterfalls and is a powerful display of how water can change the shape of the land.

![Mountain icon] **LAND REGIONS** Most of Africa is a high, flat plateau. There are few mountains. The Sahara and the Kalahari are its largest deserts. Rainforests grow along the Equator. Grasslands, called savannas, cover much of the rest of the continent.

![Water icon] **WATER** The Nile and the Congo are Africa's longest rivers. Most of Africa's largest lakes are in the Great Rift Valley.

![Climate icon] **CLIMATE** The Equator crosses Africa's middle, so many places on the continent are hot. It is always wet in the rainforests. Much of the rest of Africa has wet and dry seasons.

![Plants icon] **PLANTS** Thorny trees called acacias provide food and shade for grassland animals. Date palms grow around desert water holes. Mahogany is one of many kinds of rainforest trees.

![Animals icon] **ANIMALS** Africa has many different kinds of animals, such as elephants, lions, and gorillas. Some of the animals that live in Africa are shown here.

Acacia trees are common in the African savanna. The trees send roots down as far as 200 feet (61 m) to reach water sources beneath the dry grasslands.

S

Map Key

![Mountain symbol] Mountain
![Desert symbol] Desert
![Rainforest symbol] Rainforest
![Grassland symbol] Grassland
![Wetland symbol] Wetland
![Volcano symbol] Volcano
- ■ Point of interest
- ⸜ Waterfall

0		600 miles
0		900 kilometers

Mount Kilimanjaro, the highest point in Africa, is actually a volcano. Scientists think the last time it erupted was 360,000 years ago.

The addax lives in the Sahara desert and gets the water it needs to survive from the plants that it eats.

The secretary bird lives in open savannas and grasslands south of the Sahara desert.

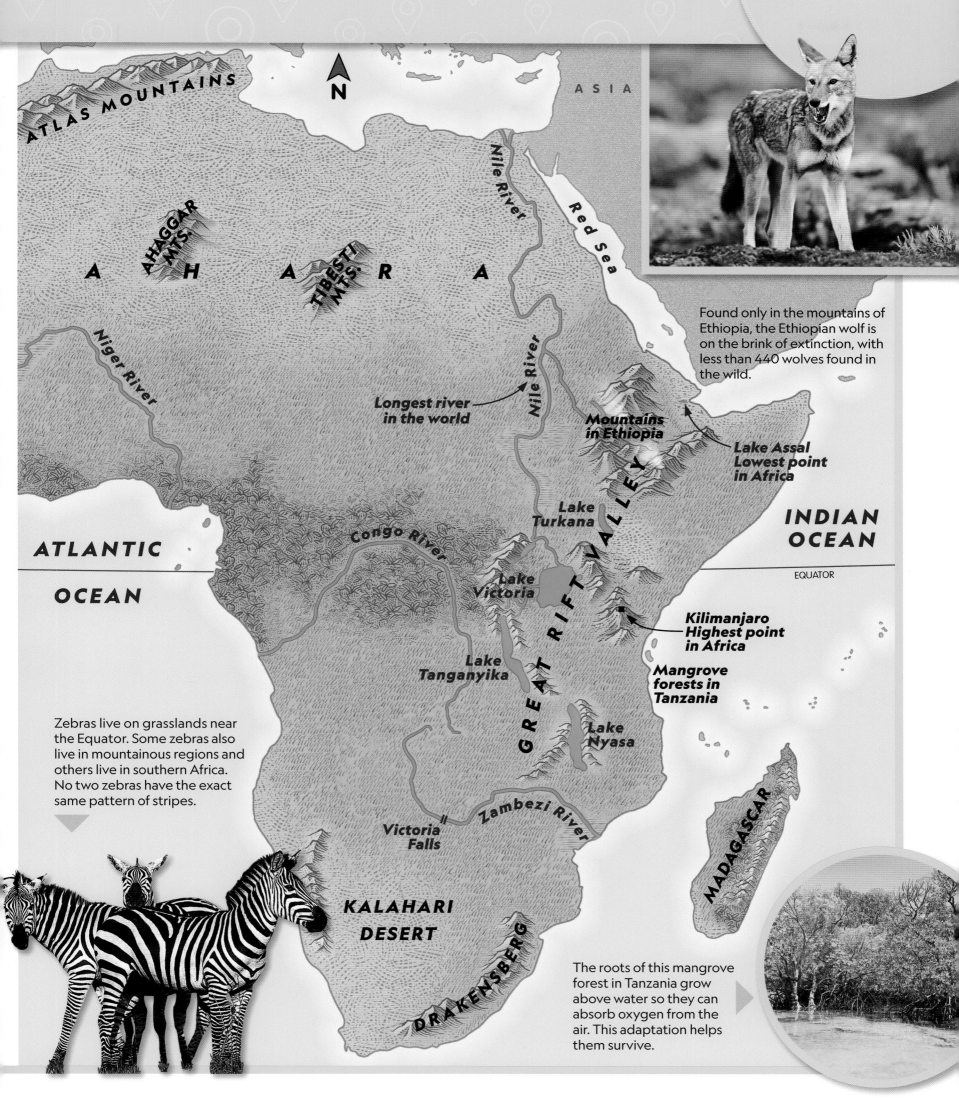

ATLAS MOUNTAINS

ASIA

N

S A H A R A

AHAGGAR MTS.

TIBESTI MTS.

Nile River

Red Sea

Niger River

Longest river in the world

Nile River

Mountains in Ethiopia

Found only in the mountains of Ethiopia, the Ethiopian wolf is on the brink of extinction, with less than 440 wolves found in the wild.

Lake Assal Lowest point in Africa

ATLANTIC

OCEAN

Congo River

Lake Turkana

INDIAN OCEAN

EQUATOR

Lake Victoria

GREAT RIFT VALLEY

Kilimanjaro Highest point in Africa

Lake Tanganyika

Mangrove forests in Tanzania

Zebras live on grasslands near the Equator. Some zebras also live in mountainous regions and others live in southern Africa. No two zebras have the exact same pattern of stripes.

Lake Nyasa

Zambezi River

MADAGASCAR

Victoria Falls

KALAHARI DESERT

DRAKENSBERG

The roots of this mangrove forest in Tanzania grow above water so they can absorb oxygen from the air. This adaptation helps them survive.

Small sailboats called feluccas carry trade goods along the Nile. The river flows north out of Lake Victoria.

Casablanca

Canary Islands (Spain)

Western Sahara (Morocco)

MAURITANIA

CABO VERDE Nouakchott ⊛

⊛ Praia Dakar ⊛ **SENEGAL**

Banjul ⊛

THE GAMBIA Bamako ⊛

Bissau ⊛ **GUINEA-BISSAU** **GUINEA**

Conakry ⊛ Yamoussoukro ⊛

Freetown ⊛

SIERRA LEONE **LIBERIA**

Monrovia ⊛

CÔTE D'IVOIRE (IVORY COAST)

COUNTRIES Several powerful kingdoms ruled over Africa until the late 1800s. Today, there are 54 independent countries. Algeria has the most land. Nigeria has the most people.

CITIES Cairo is Africa's most populous city. It is a busy port city and center of trade. But many people in Africa live in villages and on farms rather than in cities.

PEOPLE Most people in northern Africa are Arabic-speaking Muslims. Most Black Africans living south of the Sahara belong to hundreds of different ethnic groups. Many people of European origin live in major cities and in South Africa.

LANGUAGES Arabic is spoken in northern Africa. Native languages are spoken south of the Sahara. English, French, and Portuguese are the main European languages.

Workers in Côte d'Ivoire, the world's largest cocoa producer, gather cocoa pods. The pods are used to make chocolate.

Students in Kenya study the country's two official languages, Swahili and English.

The Sphinx and the pyramid behind it were built by people who lived in Egypt thousands of years ago.

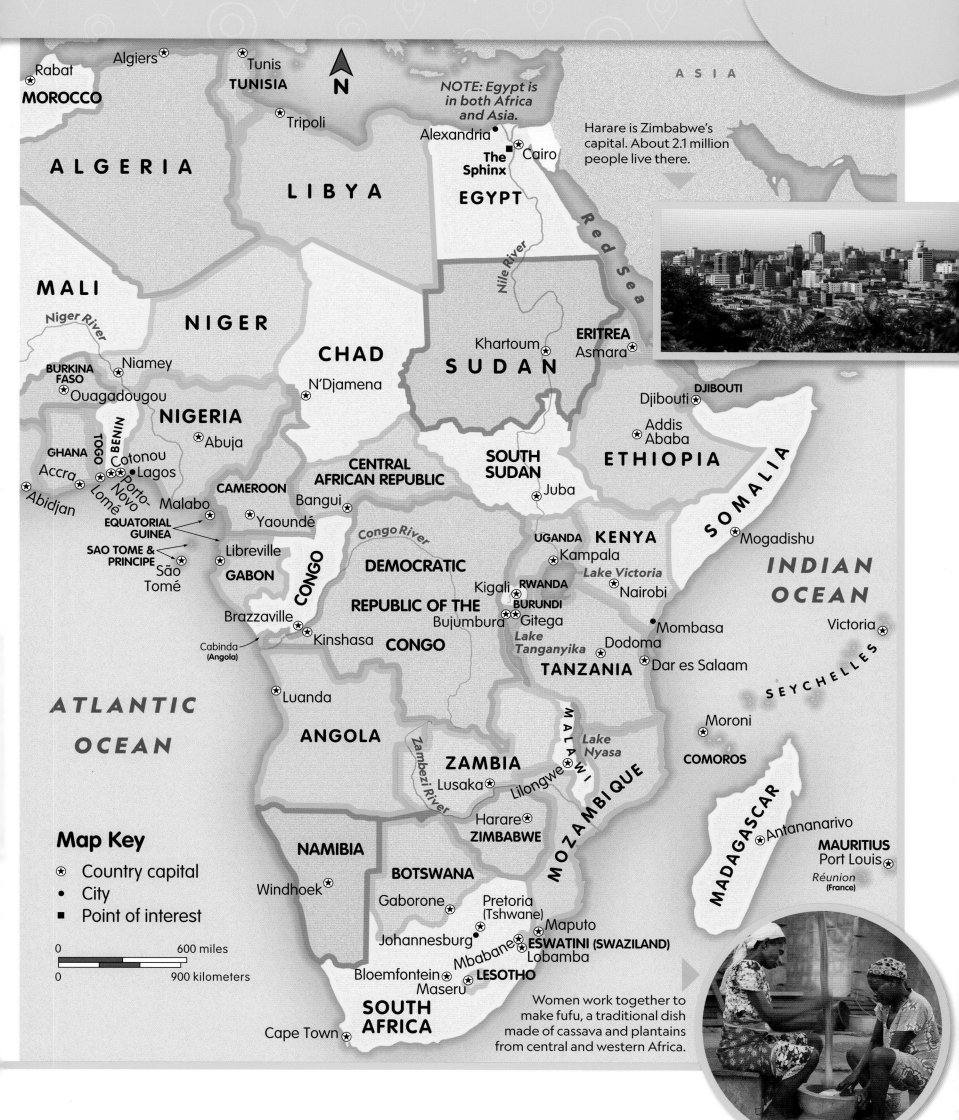

Rabat
⊛ MOROCCO

Algiers ⊛

⊛ Tunis
TUNISIA

⊛ Tripoli

NOTE: Egypt is in both Africa and Asia.

ASIA

Alexandria ⊛
The ■ Sphinx
⊛ Cairo

Harare is Zimbabwe's capital. About 2.1 million people live there.

A L G E R I A

L I B Y A

EGYPT

Red Sea

M A L I

Niger River

N I G E R

C H A D

N'Djamena ⊛

Khartoum ⊛

S U D A N

Nile River

ERITREA
Asmara ⊛

DJIBOUTI
Djibouti ⊛

BURKINA FASO
Niamey ⊛

Ouagadougou ⊛

NIGERIA

Abuja ⊛

GHANA
Accra ⊛
TOGO
BENIN
Cotonou
Porto-Novo
Lomé
Abidjan ⊛

Lagos ●

CENTRAL AFRICAN REPUBLIC

SOUTH SUDAN

Juba ⊛

Addis Ababa ⊛

ETHIOPIA

S O M A L I A

Mogadishu ⊛

Malabo ⊛

CAMEROON
Bangui ⊛

EQUATORIAL GUINEA
Yaoundé ⊛

Congo River

UGANDA
Kampala ⊛

KENYA

Lake Victoria

Nairobi ⊛

INDIAN OCEAN

SAO TOME & PRINCIPE
São Tomé ⊛

Libreville ⊛

GABON
CONGO

DEMOCRATIC
REPUBLIC OF THE

Kigali ⊛
RWANDA
BURUNDI
Bujumbura ⊛
Gitega ⊛

Mombasa ●

Victoria ⊛

Brazzaville ⊛
Kinshasa ⊛

CONGO

Lake Tanganyika

Dodoma ⊛
Dar es Salaam ⊛

SEYCHELLES

Cabinda (Angola)

TANZANIA

ATLANTIC OCEAN

Luanda ⊛

ANGOLA

Zambezi River

ZAMBIA
Lusaka ⊛

MALAWI
Lake Nyasa
Lilongwe ⊛

Moroni ⊛

COMOROS

MOZAMBIQUE

MADAGASCAR
Antananarivo ⊛

MAURITIUS
Port Louis ⊛

Map Key
⊛ Country capital
● City
■ Point of interest

0   600 miles
0   900 kilometers

NAMIBIA

Harare ⊛
ZIMBABWE

Windhoek ⊛

BOTSWANA

Gaborone ⊛

Pretoria (Tshwane) ⊛

Maputo ⊛

Réunion (France)

Johannesburg ●

Mbabane ⊛
Lobamba ⊛
ESWATINI (SWAZILAND)

Bloemfontein ⊛
Maseru ⊛
LESOTHO

SOUTH AFRICA

Cape Town ●

Women work together to make fufu, a traditional dish made of cassava and plantains from central and western Africa.

AUSTRALIA AND OCEANIA

Australia and Oceania lie south of the Equator in the Southern Hemisphere. Because of this location, Australia is known as the land "down under," as in down under the Equator. Thousands of islands and the larger countries of New Zealand and Papua New Guinea are also found in this part of the world. Because this area is made up of ocean islands, there is a strong connection between the people and the sea.

Found only in Australia, the platypus dives under the water to eat insects, shellfish, and worms.

A cable car in Wellington, New Zealand, carries passengers up a hillside. Wellington is the capital city of New Zealand.

The Three Sisters rock formation is a stunning site in the Blue Mountains of Australia. These mountains are part of the Great Dividing Range.

M I

Yap Islands

A S I A

New Guinea

Arafura Sea

Timor Sea

Great Sandy Desert

Uluru (Ayers Rock)

Great Artesian Basin

A U S T R A L I A

Great Victoria Desert

Lake Eyre Lowest point in Australia & Oceania

INDIAN OCEAN

 LAND REGIONS Australia and Oceania land regions range from the dry, sandy deserts of western Australia to the lush, tropical ocean islands of Micronesia, Melanesia, and Polynesia.

 WATER Made up entirely of islands, this region of the world is dominated by water.

 CLIMATE The climate of Australia and Oceania is determined by the size and location of each landmass. Much of Australia is very dry and warm all year. However, southern Australia can be cold in the winter. Most of Oceania's islands lie in the tropical zone—an area of Earth that is warm year-round.

PLANTS Eucalyptus and acacia trees make up the most common types of forests in Australia. Coconut palms and mangroves are common throughout the rest of Oceania.

 ANIMALS Australia is known for the many unusual animals that live there, such as marsupials that carry their young in pouches on their bellies. There are many birds in Oceania, including seabirds and colorful birds of paradise.

Moss covers trees and logs in a forest in Tasmania. This island has a much wetter climate than most of mainland Australia.

Kiwis are flightless birds native to New Zealand that have feathers that look more like hair or fur.

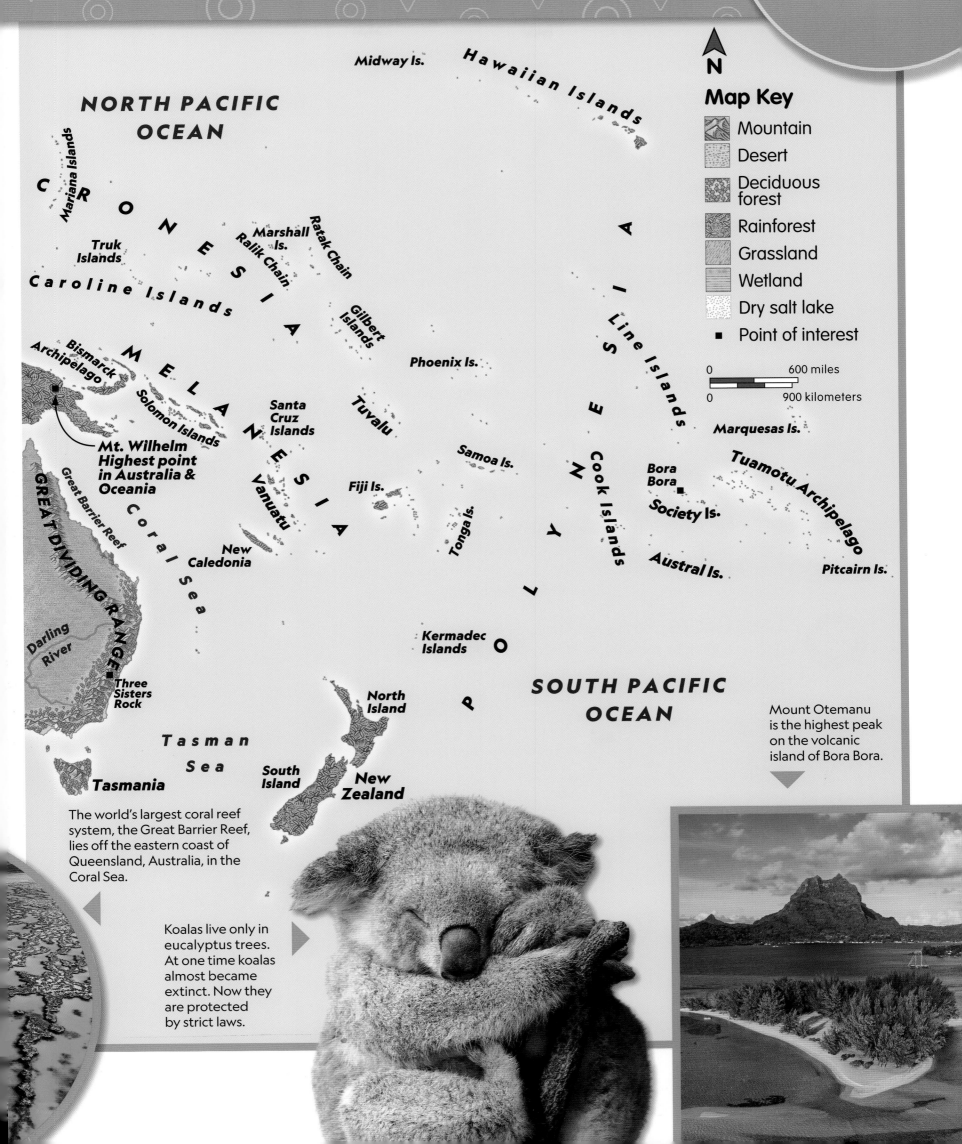

NORTH PACIFIC
OCEAN

Midway Is.   Hawaiian Islands

Map Key

- Mountain
- Desert
- Deciduous forest
- Rainforest
- Grassland
- Wetland
- Dry salt lake
- ▪ Point of interest

0   600 miles
0   900 kilometers

MICRONESIA

Mariana Islands

Truk Islands

Marshall Is.

Ralik Chain   Ratak Chain

Caroline Islands

Gilbert Islands

Phoenix Is.

Line Islands

MELANESIA

Bismarck Archipelago

Solomon Islands

Mt. Wilhelm Highest point in Australia & Oceania

Santa Cruz Islands

Tuvalu

Marquesas Is.

Samoa Is.

Bora Bora

Tuamotu Archipelago

Vanuatu

Fiji Is.

Coral Sea

GREAT DIVIDING RANGE

Great Barrier Reef

Darling River

Three Sisters Rock

New Caledonia

Tonga Is.

Society Is.

Cook Islands

Austral Is.

POLYNESIA

Pitcairn Is.

Kermadec Islands

SOUTH PACIFIC OCEAN

Mount Otemanu is the highest peak on the volcanic island of Bora Bora.

Tasman Sea

North Island

South Island

New Zealand

Tasmania

The world's largest coral reef system, the Great Barrier Reef, lies off the eastern coast of Queensland, Australia, in the Coral Sea.

Koalas live only in eucalyptus trees. At one time koalas almost became extinct. Now they are protected by strict laws.

AUSTRALIA AND OCEANIA

Surfing is popular in Australia. There is even a suburb of Queensland's Gold Coast named Surfers Paradise.

M i

PALAU
Ngerulmud ⊛   C a

FEDERATED

A S I A

Darwin ⊙

NORTHERN TERRITORY

AUSTRALIA

WESTERN AUSTRALIA

SOUTH AUSTRALIA   Lake Eyre

⊙ Perth

Adelaide ⊙

INDIAN OCEAN

COUNTRIES Australia is the largest country in the Oceania region. The rest of this area is made up of island nations including New Zealand, Papua New Guinea, and the many islands of Micronesia, Melanesia, and Polynesia.

CITIES All the major cities of Australia are near the coast, except for the capital city, Canberra. There are many other cities peppered throughout Oceania's islands.

PEOPLE Most Australians are descendants of settlers from the United Kingdom and Ireland. Aboriginals came to Australia from Asia some 40,000 years ago. Members of many different indigenous, or native, cultures live on the islands of Oceania.

LANGUAGES The region of Oceania has more than 1,500 native languages spoken in addition to English, which is the main language spoken in Australia, New Zealand, and on many of the islands.

A didgeridoo, a traditional instrument of the Aboriginal peoples, is played before a rugby match in Australia.

Australia, New Zealand, and Papua New Guinea have large fisheries and export seafood products to places all over the world. ▶

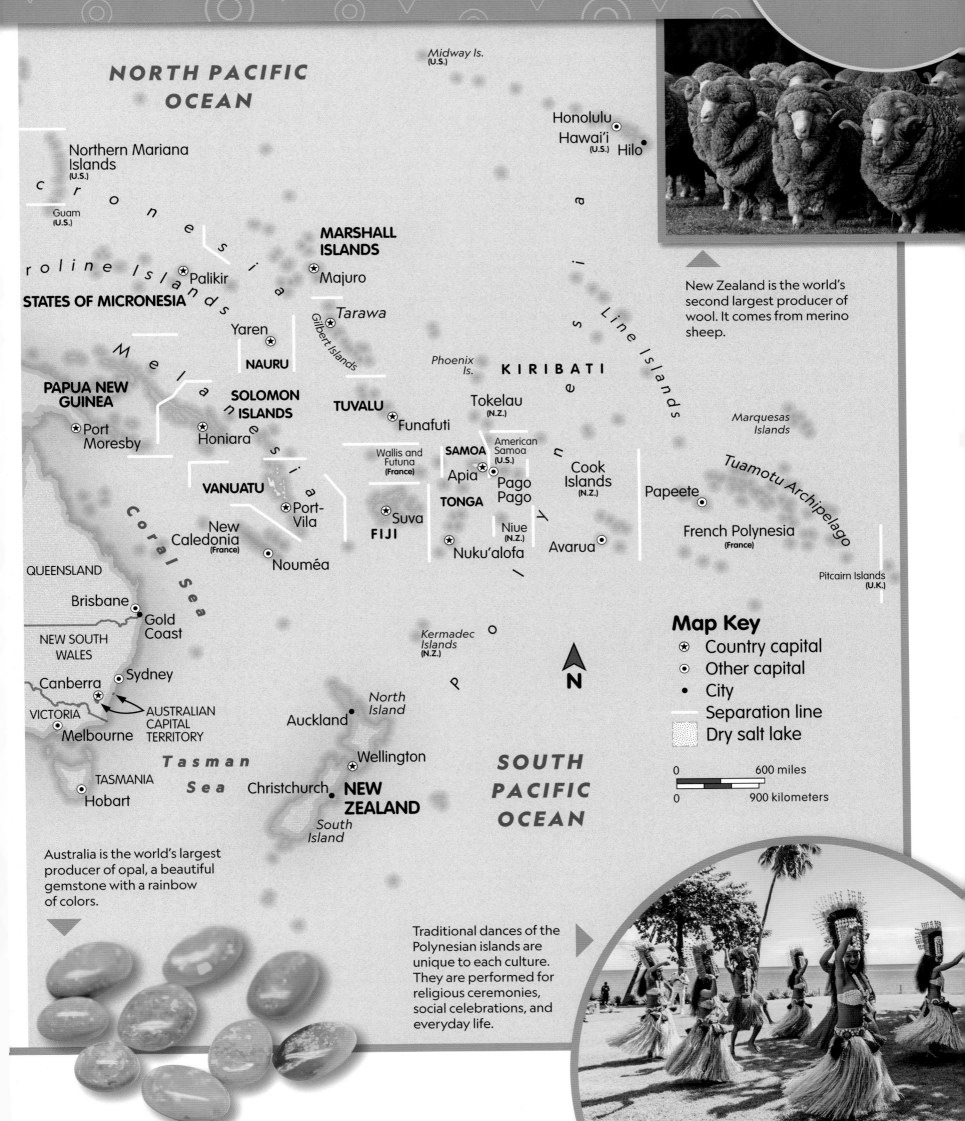

NORTH PACIFIC OCEAN

Midway Is. (U.S.)

Honolulu
Hawai'i (U.S.)
Hilo

c r o n e s i a

Northern Mariana Islands (U.S.)

Guam (U.S.)

roline Islands

⊛ Palikir

STATES OF MICRONESIA

M e l a n e s i a

PAPUA NEW GUINEA

⊛ Port Moresby

MARSHALL ISLANDS

⊛ Majuro

⊛ Tarawa

Gilbert Islands

Yaren
⊛

NAURU

SOLOMON ISLANDS

⊛ Honiara

TUVALU

⊛ Funafuti

Phoenix Is.

K I R I B A T I

Tokelau (N.Z.)

L i n e   I s l a n d s

New Zealand is the world's second largest producer of wool. It comes from merino sheep.

Marquesas Islands

M e l a n e s i a

VANUATU

⊛ Port-Vila

New Caledonia (France)

⊙ Nouméa

Wallis and Futuna (France)

⊛ Suva

FIJI

SAMOA

Apia ⊛

American Samoa (U.S.)

Pago Pago

TONGA

Niue (N.Z.)

Nuku'alofa

Cook Islands (N.Z.)

Avarua ⊙

P o l y n e s i a

Papeete ⊙

French Polynesia (France)

Tuamotu Archipelago

Pitcairn Islands (U.K.)

QUEENSLAND

C o r a l   S e a

Brisbane
Gold Coast

NEW SOUTH WALES

Canberra
Sydney
⊛
AUSTRALIAN CAPITAL TERRITORY

VICTORIA
⊙
Melbourne

T a s m a n   S e a

TASMANIA
⊙
Hobart

Auckland

North Island

Wellington
⊛
Christchurch

NEW ZEALAND

South Island

Kermadec Islands (N.Z.)

N

SOUTH PACIFIC OCEAN

Map Key
- ⊛ Country capital
- ⊙ Other capital
- • City
- ― Separation line
- ▦ Dry salt lake

0		600 miles

0		900 kilometers

Australia is the world's largest producer of opal, a beautiful gemstone with a rainbow of colors.

Traditional dances of the Polynesian islands are unique to each culture. They are performed for religious ceremonies, social celebrations, and everyday life.

ANTARCTICA

*B*rrrr! Antarctica is the coldest continent. It is the land around the South Pole and is surrounded by the very cold waters of the Southern Ocean. An ice sheet that can be two miles (3 km) thick in some places covers most of the land. Temperatures rarely get above freezing. It is also the only continent that has no countries. It has research stations but no cities. The only people here are scientists, explorers, and tourists. The largest year-round land animal on Antarctica is a wingless insect!

Weddell seals are found only in the Antarctic region of the world.

This gentoo penguin chick shows off its long tail. Gentoos have the longest tail of any penguin species.

This strong-sided ship is an icebreaker. It cuts a path through ice in the Ross Sea.

Esperanza Base

ANTARCTIC CIRCLE

ANTARCTIC

Home to only 10 families, the Esperanza Base is a village and also a research center for scientists.

Bellingshausen Sea

ELLSWORTH LAND

Amundsen Sea

LAND REGIONS The Transantarctic Mountains divide the continent into two parts. East Antarctica, where the South Pole is located, is mostly a high, flat, icy area. West Antarctica is mountainous. The Antarctic Peninsula extends like a finger toward South America. Vinson Massif is the highest peak.

WATER Most of Earth's freshwater is frozen in Antarctica's ice sheet. The ice breaks off when it meets the Southern Ocean. These huge floating chunks of ice in the ocean are called icebergs.

CLIMATE Antarctica is cold, windy, and dry. What little snow falls turns to ice. The thick ice sheet has built up over millions of years.

PLANTS Billions of tiny plants live in the surrounding oceans. Mosses and lichens grow on exposed rocks.

ANIMALS Most Antarctic animals live in the water or close to the coast. Penguins nest on the coast, while whales and tiny shrimplike krill live in the ocean.

Many animals in this region mainly eat tiny Antarctic krill.

The Adélie penguin is one of two penguin species that only live on the Antarctic continent.

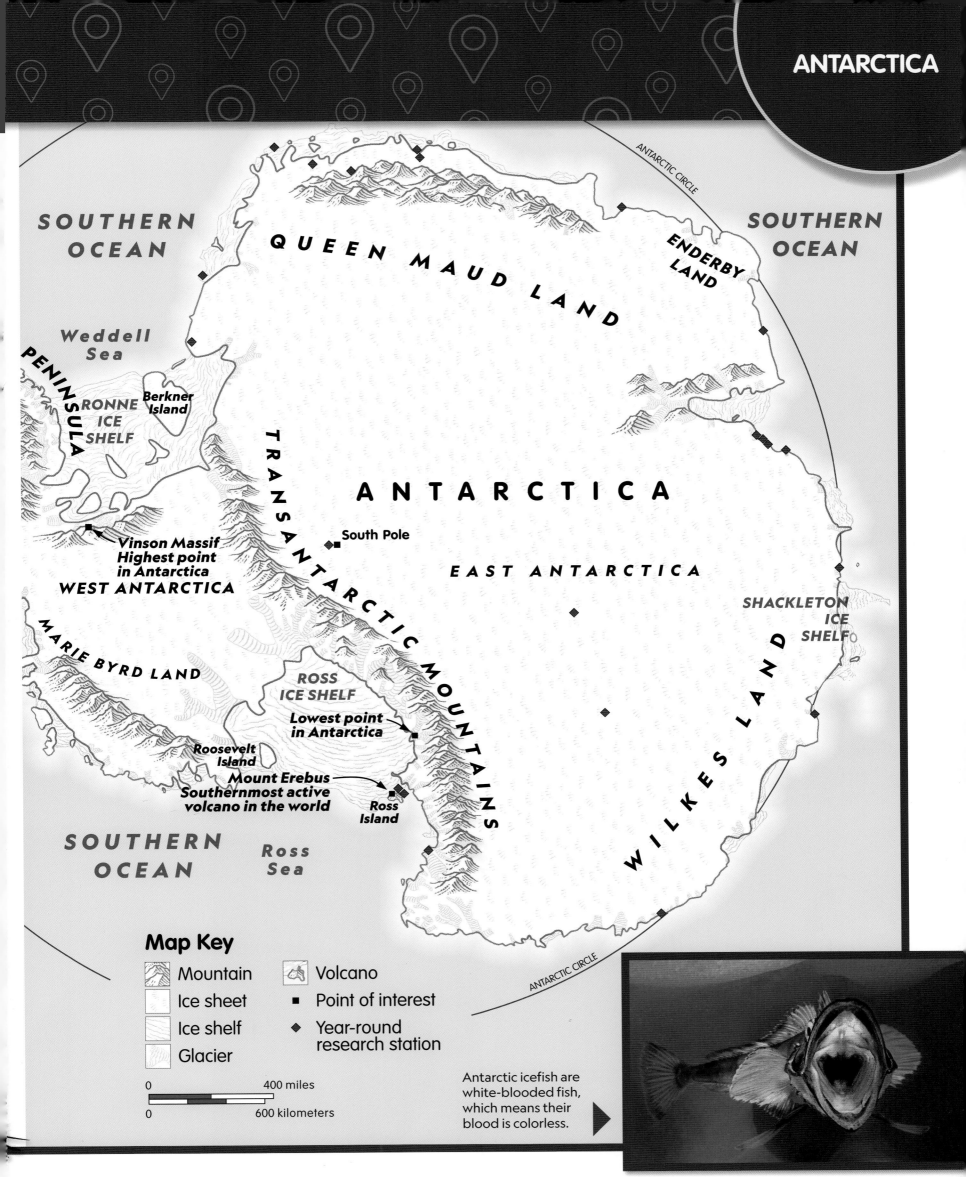

SOUTHERN OCEAN

SOUTHERN OCEAN

ANTARCTIC CIRCLE

QUEEN MAUD LAND

ENDERBY LAND

Weddell Sea

PENINSULA

RONNE ICE SHELF

Berkner Island

TRANSANTARCTIC MOUNTAINS

ANTARCTICA

South Pole

EAST ANTARCTICA

Vinson Massif
Highest point
in Antarctica
WEST ANTARCTICA

SHACKLETON ICE SHELF

MARIE BYRD LAND

ROSS ICE SHELF

Lowest point
in Antarctica

Roosevelt Island

WILKES LAND

Mount Erebus
Southernmost active
volcano in the world

Ross Island

SOUTHERN OCEAN

Ross Sea

ANTARCTIC CIRCLE

Map Key

- Mountain
- Ice sheet
- Ice shelf
- Glacier
- Volcano
- Point of interest
- Year-round research station

0   400 miles

0   600 kilometers

Antarctic icefish are
white-blooded fish,
which means their
blood is colorless.

WORLD AT A GLANCE

Land

The Continents, Largest to Smallest

1. **Asia:** 17,208,000 sq mi (44,570,000 sq km)
2. **Africa:** 11,608,000 sq mi (30,065,000 sq km)
3. **North America:** 9,449,000 sq mi (24,474,000 sq km)
4. **South America:** 6,880,000 sq mi (17,819,000 sq km)
5. **Antarctica:** 5,100,000 sq mi (13,209,000 sq km)
6. **Europe:** 3,841,000 sq mi (9,947,000 sq km)
7. **Australia:** 2,970,000 sq mi (7,692,000 sq km)

People

More than 7.8 billion people live on Earth in almost 200 countries. More than half of the world's people live in Asia. A little more than half of the global population lives in towns and cities.

Five Largest Countries by Number of People (2021 data)

1. **China, Asia:** 1,397,898,000 people
2. **India, Asia:** 1,339,331,000 people
3. **United States, North America:** 334,998,000 people
4. **Indonesia, Asia:** 275,122,000 people
5. **Pakistan, Asia:** 238,181,000 people

Ten Largest Cities* by Number of People (2021 data)

1. **Tokyo, Japan (Asia):** 37,340,000 people
2. **Delhi, India (Asia):** 31,181,000 people
3. **Shanghai, China (Asia):** 27,796,000 people
4. **São Paulo, Brazil (South America):** 22,237,000 people
5. **Mexico City, Mexico (North America):** 21,919,000 people
6. **Dhaka, Bangladesh (Asia):** 21,741,000 people
7. **Cairo, Egypt (Africa):** 21,323,000 people
8. **Beijing, China (Asia):** 20,897,000 people
9. **Mumbai, India (Asia):** 20,668,000 people
10. **Osaka, Japan (Asia):** 19,111,000 people

*Figures are for metropolitan areas.

Water

The Oceans, Largest to Smallest

1. **Pacific Ocean:** 65,100,000 sq mi (168,600,000 sq km)
2. **Atlantic Ocean:** 33,100,000 sq mi (85,600,000 sq km)
3. **Indian Ocean:** 27,500,000 sq mi (71,200,000 sq km)
4. **Southern Ocean:** 8,500,000 sq mi (21,900,000 sq km)
5. **Arctic Ocean:** 6,100,000 sq mi (15,700,000 sq km)

Highest, Tallest, Longest, Largest

The numbers below show their locations on the map.

1 **Highest Mountain on a Continent**
Mount Everest, in Asia: 29,032 ft (8,849 m)

2 **Tallest Waterfall**
Angel Falls, in South America: 3,212 ft (979 m)

3 **Largest Island**
Greenland, borders the Arctic and Atlantic Oceans: 836,000 sq mi (2,166,000 sq km)

4 **Largest Ocean**
Pacific Ocean: 65,100,000 sq mi (168,600,000 sq km)

5 **Longest River**
Nile River, in Africa: 4,160 mi (6,695 km)

6 **Largest Freshwater Lake**
Lake Superior, in North America: 31,700 sq mi (82,100 sq km)

7 **Largest Saltwater Lake**
Caspian Sea, in Europe and Asia: 143,200 sq mi (371,000 sq km)

8 **Largest Coral Reef Ecosystem**
Great Barrier Reef, in Australia: 134,000 sq mi (348,300 sq km)

9 **Largest Hot Desert**
Sahara, in Africa: 3,475,000 sq mi (9,000,000 sq km)

10 **Largest Ice Desert**
Antarctica: 5,100,000 sq mi (13,209,000 sq km)

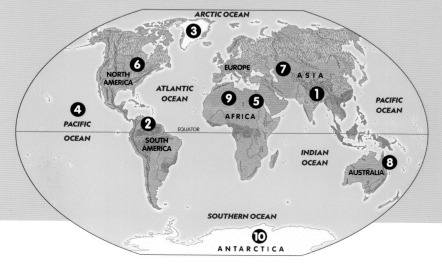

GLOSSARY

adaptation a physical characteristic or a behavior of a plant or animal that helps it to survive

capital city the seat of government for a country, state, or province

city a settled place where people work in jobs other than farming

colonist a person who settles in a new place, often to claim land for another country

coral reef a stony formation in warm, shallow ocean water that is made up of the skeletons of tiny sea animals called corals

country a place that has boundaries, a name, a flag, and a government that is the highest world authority over the land and the people who live there

decade a period of 10 years

environment the world around you, including people, cities, plants and animals, air, water—everything

erosion the movement of soil, dirt, and rocks by wind or water

ethnic group people who share a common ancestry, language, beliefs, and traditions

euro the official currency of the European Union

European Union an organization of 27 European countries (Austria,* Belgium,* Bulgaria, Croatia, Cyprus,* Czechia [Czech Republic], Denmark, Estonia,* Finland,* France,* Germany,* Greece,* Hungary, Ireland,* Italy,* Latvia,* Lithuania,* Luxembourg,* Malta,* Netherlands,* Poland, Portugal,* Romania, Slovakia,* Slovenia,* Spain,* and Sweden as of July 2021. Countries marked with an asterisk (*) use the euro as their official currency.

export a good or a service provided that is sold to other countries

extinct a species of plant or animal that can no longer be found living on Earth

glacier a large, slow-moving mass of ice. Glaciers that cover huge areas are called ice sheets, or continental glaciers.

lichen a plantlike organism that is part alga and part fungus and that usually lives where few plants can survive

mosses nonflowering, low-growing green plants that grow on rocks and trees

plains large areas of mainly flat land often covered with grasses

plateau a large, mainly level area of high land

populous having a large population, or number of people

province a unit of government similar to a state

state a unit of government that takes up a specific area within a country, as in one of the 50 large political units in the United States

steppe a Russian word for the grasslands that stretch from eastern Europe into Asia

taiga a Russian word for the scattered coniferous forests that grow in cold, northern regions

tributary a river or stream that flows into a larger river

uplifting upward movement of the surface of Earth

weathering the breaking down of Earth's surface by wind, water, gases in the atmosphere, plants, and animals

METRIC CONVERSIONS FOUND IN THIS ATLAS

CONVERSIONS TO METRIC MEASUREMENTS

WHEN YOU KNOW	MULTIPLY BY	TO FIND
INCHES (IN)	2.54	CENTIMETERS (CM)
FEET (FT)	0.30	METERS (M)
MILES (MI)	1.61	KILOMETERS (KM)
SQUARE MILES (SQ MI)	2.59	SQUARE KILOMETERS (SQ KM)
POUNDS (LB)	0.45	KILOGRAMS (KG)

CONVERSIONS FROM METRIC MEASUREMENTS

WHEN YOU KNOW	MULTIPLY BY	TO FIND
CENTIMETERS (CM)	0.39	INCHES (IN)
METERS (M)	3.28	FEET (FT)
KILOMETERS (KM)	0.62	MILES (MI)
SQUARE KILOMETERS (SQ KM)	0.39	SQUARE MILES (SQ MI)
KILOGRAMS (KG)	2.20	POUNDS (LB)

INDEX

Pictures and the text that describes them have their page numbers printed in **bold** type.

First Edition Copyright © 1999 National Geographic Society
Updated © 2005, 2011 National Geographic Society
Updated © 2019, 2022 National Geographic Partners, LLC.
All rights reserved. Reproduction of the whole or any part of the contents without written permission from the publisher is prohibited.

NATIONAL GEOGRAPHIC and Yellow Border Design are trademarks of the National Geographic Society, used under license.

Since 1888, the National Geographic Society has funded more than 14,000 research, conservation, education, and storytelling projects around the world. National Geographic Partners distributes a portion of the funds it receives from your purchase to National Geographic Society to support programs including the conservation of animals and their habitats. To learn more, visit natgeo.com/info.

For more information, visit nationalgeographic.com, call 1-877-873-6846, or write to the following address:

National Geographic Partners, LLC
1145 17th Street NW
Washington, DC 20036-4688 U.S.A.

For librarians and teachers: nationalgeographic.com/books/librarians-and-educators

More for kids from National Geographic: natgeokids.com

National Geographic Kids magazine inspires children to explore their world with fun yet educational articles on animals, science, nature, and more. Using fresh storytelling and amazing photography, *Nat Geo Kids* shows kids ages 6 to 14 the fascinating truth about the world—and why they should care. **natgeo.com/subscribe**

For rights or permissions inquiries, please contact National Geographic Books Subsidiary Rights: bookrights@natgeo.com

Designed by Kathryn Robbins

Trade paperback ISBN: 978-1-4263-7334-3
Hardcover ISBN: 978-1-4263-7242-1
Reinforced library binding ISBN: 978-1-4263-7335-0

Acknowledgments
The publisher would like to thank everyone who worked to make this book come together: Skye Powers-Kaminski, writer and geography educator; Angela Modany, associate editor; Hilary Andrews, associate photo editor; Mike McNey, senior cartographer; Maureen J. Flynn, map editor; and Anne LeongSon and Gus Tello, associate designers.

Printed in Hong Kong
22/PPHK/1

There's always more ...
TO EXPLORE!

National Geographic Kids has the perfect atlas for kids of every age, from preschool through high school—all with the latest age-appropriate facts, maps, images, and more.

The atlas series is designed to grow as kids grow, adding more depth and relevant material at every level to help them stay curious about the world and to succeed at school and in life!

AGES 7-10

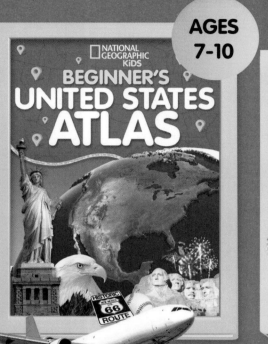

AGES 11-14

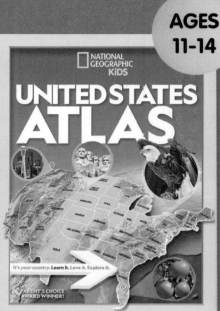